party**vegan**

fabulous, fun food for
every occasion

robinrobertson

WILEY

john wiley & sons, inc.

Published by John Wiley & Sons, Inc., Hoboken, New Jersey
Published simultaneously in Canada

For general information on our other products and services or for technical support, please contact our
Customer Care Department within the United States at (800) 762-2974, outside the United States at
(317) 572-3993 or fax (317) 572-4002.

Wiley also publishes its books in a variety of electronic formats. Some content that appears in print may
not be available in electronic books. For more information about Wiley products, visit our web site at
www.wiley.com.

Library of Congress Cataloging-in-Publication Data:
Robertson, Robin (Robin G.)
    Party vegan: fabulous, fun food for every occasion / Robin Robertson.
        p. cm.
    Includes index.
    ISBN 978-0-470-47223-1 (pbk.) ; 978-0-470-94358-8 (ebook); 978-0-470-94359-5 (ebook)
    1. Vegan cookery. 2. Entertaining. I. Title.
    TX837.R62497143 2010
    641.5'636 — dc22

                                    2009042656

Book design by Debbie Glasserman
Printed in the United States of America
10 9 8 7 6 5 4 3 2 1

This book is dedicated to
party animals everywhere
who don't serve animals
at their parties.

contents

anytime gatherings

holiday gatherings

acknowledgments

Working on this book was a special joy because it brought back wonderful memories of parties past and, most especially, the friends and family with whom I shared such good times. For those people, and those memories, I am grateful. Of course, it inspired new reasons to celebrate, too!

My deepest gratitude goes to the finest trio of recipe testers in the galaxy: Tami Noyes, Jenna Patton, and Russell Patton, who tested each and every recipe in this book with care and enthusiasm. Their dedication and zest for cooking is astonishing. Thanks for making Thanksgiving dinner in July and testing picnic food when there was snow on the ground.

A special thank you to my husband, Jon, who helps to make each day a reason to celebrate.

I also want to thank the talented team at John Wiley & Sons, especially my editor, Linda Ingroia. A big thanks to Alda Trabucchi, the production editor, as well as editorial assistant Rebecca Scherm and Suzanne Sunwoo, the cover designer. Designer Debbie Glasserman gets credit for the lively look of the book. Thanks also to my long-time agent, Stacey Glick of Dystel & Goderich Literary Management.

introduction

Everyone loves a party, and most of us entertain at least a few times a year, whether it's having the relatives over for a holiday meal, or friends gathered for nibbles and board games. In *Party Vegan* you'll find a wide variety of creative menus and great-tasting recipes at your fingertips for every occasion. In addition, the recipes in this book have the benefit of being healthy and accessible to everyone, without compromising on flavor.

From a certain perspective, you could say my life has been one big party. When I was growing up, my parents were always entertaining. Some of my earliest memories include festive holiday meals and all the cooking and preparation that my mother put into them. After Christmas dinner, my parents would host a holiday open house, in which family and friends would stream in and out all day to share food, drink, and conversation.

When I was very young, I would delight in crashing my parents' Saturday night poker parties where they played penny ante with relatives and neighbors. The only thing more inviting than that mound of shiny pennies on the card table was the bountiful spread of sandwich fixings my mom had put out for refreshments.

Like most families, we had other reasons to party throughout the year, including birthday celebrations, holidays, and cookouts. The food my mother prepared on these occasions was sometimes simple and other times fancy, but always plentiful and delicious.

Years later, as a chef and caterer, I was the one putting out the party food for other people's events. Instead of the homey fare that my mother served family and friends, I was creating elegant upscale food for clients' parties in the stately mansions of Charleston, South Carolina. The pleasure of serving delicious food was instilled in me by my mother and refined during my years in professional food service. To this day, I enjoy entertaining friends and family and take great pleasure in making festive food look and taste beautiful.

To many people, the thought of hosting a special meal or party produces a stress reaction, and not without reason. Depending on the occasion and the number of people attending, there are endless details needing attention, not the least of which is preparing vegan food that even omnivorous guests will enjoy. As a result, hosting a party where the goal is to relax and have fun can often be one of the least relaxing events you can undertake, unless you have a plan. And that's what this book is all about.

Although there was a world of difference between my parents' get-togethers in our modest Pennsylvania home and the lavish parties I catered in the mansions of Charleston, South Carolina, both had two specific things in common that spelled success: careful planning and advance preparation. Whether preparing snacks for a few friends or hosting a sophisticated soiree, I've learned time and again that if you plan well and prepare as much as possible in advance, you can actually enjoy your own party along with your guests. And if you're able to have fun and relax, your guests will enjoy your party all the more.

Party Vegan isn't just for vegans, but also for vegetarians and health-conscious omnivores, and anyone looking for healthy and innovative menus and recipes. Because the recipes contain no dairy, cholesterol, or saturated fat, those with special dietary needs such as lactose intolerance or high cholesterol will find lots of reasons to party in this book. With its wide variety of delicious recipes for appetizers, main dishes, desserts, and more, *Party Vegan* has something for everyone.

With more than 140 delicious recipes, helpful tips, and informative sidebars, *Party Vegan* delivers new ways to make the most of your special times with creative menus and dazzling fare that tastes great but requires only a minimum of effort.

Party Vegan offers more than just recipes—it's filled with menus that will make entertaining easy from now on, whether you're cooking for holiday meals, kids' parties, cookouts, cocktail parties, buffets, or potlucks. There's even a chapter on how to prepare food for large gatherings such as weddings and reunions, and a guide on how to feed a large crowd.

Party Vegan is easy to use because the chapters are arranged according to the type of event you're planning, offering more than twenty-five year-round menus for various occasions, holidays, and themes, from a Super Bowl party to Thanksgiving dinner, with complete menu strategies and recipes for each event. Included in the book is a day-by-day countdown of what needs to be done and when. You will also find tips on how to round out your menus with high-quality convenience foods to help take the pressure off the cook and a timetable for organizing your time leading up to the event. Best of all, most of the recipes can be prepared in advance, so you can relax and enjoy the party yourself (look for the Make-Ahead symbol). Many of the recipes can be made in under 20 minutes; for these you'll see the Quick & Easy symbol . *Party Vegan* makes it easy to understand why preparing vegan food is the perfect choice for any gathering. Perhaps most important, the recipes in this book don't need to be reserved for special occasions or used within the confines of an entire menu. You can enjoy any of the recipes any time you choose.

To me, every time I cook is a celebration of life. As long as people gather in the spirit of friendship and goodwill, then even the simplest fare can be wonderful and memorable. And no matter how spectacular the food, the most important thing is to have a good time. Now, let's party!

Every year, home cooks all over America tackle the job of throwing a party. They plan special meals for sit-down dinners, stand-up buffets, holidays, celebrations, cookouts, and picnics. There's always a reason to celebrate and share good food. However, whether it's a child's birthday party, Thanksgiving dinner, or a cocktail party for friends, some people stress out about what to prepare, let alone the work involved. They also puzzle over planning menus that everyone will enjoy, from vegans, to vegetarians, to meat-eaters, as well as people who are on special diets.

In *Party Vegan*, my goal is to take the stress work (and guesswork) out of entertaining, with easy and innovative menus, flavorful recipes, an easy-to-follow countdown, and guidelines and tips for stress-free entertaining. Because these recipes contain no animal products, they can be eaten by everyone on your invitation list, yet they are delicious enough to satisfy any palate.

People often skip the introductory material in cookbooks and get right to the recipes; however, you'll turn yourself into an expert party planner by reading this chapter and understanding the party-planning strategies that I learned while working as a professional chef and caterer.

start with a plan

The success of any party depends upon the steps you take leading up to it—the planning, cooking, and other preparation involved. Between the time you invite your guests and when they take their first savory bites, there's a lot of ground to cover, and that's what this chapter is all about.

In planning any gathering, it's important to find your comfort zone regarding the type of party you want and the food you will be serving. Pleasing your guests and having fun yourself are also important—the food doesn't have to be fancy for people to enjoy getting together. From my own experience, the people that gathered at my parents' home when I was a child were having a lot more fun than some I've since observed at swanky (and sometimes stuffy) cocktail parties that I catered. By following the guidelines in this book, you can have it all: good food, great company, and a wonderful, stress-free party.

party basics

I use "party" as a general term for anything from a casual gathering of a few friends to a multicourse holiday dinner. The fact is, whenever people and food come together—that's a party to me.

In terms of how the food is served, there are three basic presentations: plated, buffet, or grazing, or some variation on all three. To decide which is best for you, remember that your party should reflect who you are. Do you prefer a more casual style in which you spend as little time as possible in the kitchen? Or are you a china-and-linens kind of person who enjoys preparing elaborate recipes and fussing with details? The menus and recipes in this book allow you to do either with style and flair. All you have to do is zero in on what you enjoy and feel comfortable with and the rest will fall into place.

■ PLATED SIT-DOWN DINNER: If you're serving a sit-down meal, make sure to plan it only for the number of people that you can seat comfortably at your dining table. For me, that means six, although for you it may mean four or eight.

The plated sit-down meal is served formally, which adds an air of elegance to the event. You plate each course like it's a work of art and serve it in an intimate and decorous atmosphere. This type of celebration requires the most work on your part.

■ FAMILY-STYLE SIT-DOWN DINNER: An easier way to serve a sit-down meal that involves less fuss is a variation of the plated sit-down dinner in which the food is served family-style in bowls on the dining table and guests pass the food themselves. Because this approach allows people to serve themselves, it is easier and less work than plating everyone's food yourself. If your dining table can't accommodate a number of serving bowls and platters, however, you can arrange the serving dishes on a buffet or sideboard, or set up a separate table for the food, possibly even arranging your serving dishes on the kitchen counter, depending on how your kitchen is laid out. Allowing people to serve themselves also makes the atmosphere more casual, gives people something to do, and allows them to feel more at ease, since they can control their own portion sizes and food choices.

■ BUFFET: When serving more than four to six people, I always opt for the buffet. If you are serving a large crowd, the buffet makes sense. Keep in mind, however, that unless you have enough tables to accommodate everyone, the food choices should be limited to those that can be eaten as pickup food or with just a fork. Otherwise, your guests may find it difficult to balance a plate of food while trying to cut into anything larger than bite-size. A buffet can feature particular food types, such as appetizers, sandwiches, or desserts.

GRAZING MENU: Beyond the served and buffet sit-down meals is the grazing menu, where all the food is pickup—no forks needed. A grazing party or appetizer buffet can be as simple or as elaborate as you like. It is the easiest kind of party and can consist of little more than dips, chips, party mix, and other snacks along with appropriate beverages. On the other end of the spectrum is a fancy alternative to the grazing menu, what people often think of as a cocktail party, where gorgeous hors d'oeuvres are arranged just-so on serving platters.

If you want your guests to do more than graze, but you don't want to prepare an elaborate seated meal, then an informal buffet is the way to go. It can be brunch, lunch, or dinner, indoors or outdoors. Just set out the food buffet-style and the guests will serve themselves. If you want to throw a fancy party that's not as elaborate as a seated dinner party, consider hosting an elegant appetizer party. Although preparing some of the food may be a bit more work-intensive, it's still easier than a dinner party because all the food is put out at once and, again, the guests serve themselves.

theme parties

You can create a theme where you put your own spin on a party, whether you're serving a sit-down dinner, a buffet, or a grazing menu. Perhaps the most well-known theme party is the costume party, although Halloween isn't the only time of year to have one. Any time is a good time for a costume party; all you have to do is provide a theme. For example, ask your guests to dress like hippies and play sixties music all night or choose another era, depending on the age or interests of the crowd. Hosting a beach party in the middle of January is a great way to beat the winter blahs.

Certain theme parties are obvious: the birthday party, the baby shower, the graduation party. But sometimes you just feel like having a few people over. For those times, there's no real need for a theme, but I've found that if you can think of a fun reason for the gathering, it can liven things up and make the party more memorable. A few of my favorite theme parties that I hosted in recent years are described on page 4. None involved elaborate preparation (two didn't involve any cooking at all), yet they were all great fun and enjoyed by everyone who attended.

3

it'saparty!

Chocolate Tasting

Food writing can definitely have its perks. For a time, I wrote a product comparison column for *VegNews Magazine.* In one particular issue, the subject was vegan chocolate. With boxes of delectable chocolates arriving daily from various companies, it was a decadent embarrassment of riches. I decided to host a chocolate-tasting party and invited several friends. It was winter, so we set up a large table near the fireplace. I plated the various brands of chocolate and assigned each a code so no one knew what brand they were eating. I provided everyone with a corresponding sheet on which they could write their comments. Along with the chocolate, I put out a platter of ripe fruit to complement the chocolate and some plain crackers for clearing the palate. I also offered a choice of beverages designed to enhance the chocolate experience. The evening was a huge success. Everyone had great fun posing as food critics and their comments were helpful to me the next day when writing my column. Other than slicing a few pears and opening some wine, no food preparation was required. Entertaining doesn't get much easier than that.

Movie Night

For another party, my husband and I brought together several friends who shared an interest in corny old science fiction movies. The night we screened the 1962 movie *The Day of the Triffids,* I only served a few snacks, but included a bowl of trail mix containing a variety of oddly shaped and colored snack foods that I had bought at an Asian market. I dubbed it "Triffid Chow" and it was the hit of the evening. Total work involved (after shopping): five minutes.

A "Toast" Party

Sometimes a whimsical idea can develop into a unique theme for a party. One year, I was planning to invite some friends over for a casual New Year's Eve party. To toast the New Year, I got tracking on the word "toast" and thought it would be fun if everything served related to that word. When friends asked what they could bring, I explained my theme: "anything to toast or toast with or that otherwise relates to the word 'toast.'" For my part, I prepared a champagne punch with which to toast all my friends throughout the evening, which led up to the special champagne toast at midnight. The menu included baguettes and a few rustic loaves for toasting as the base for crostini and bruschetta, along with several toppings to spoon onto them. One friend brought a panini press, and we used it to make wonderful toasted sandwiches. Others brought champagne and alternative bottles of bubbly that helped keep the toasts flowing. Someone brought vegan marshmallows to toast in the fire-place, with which we promptly made a dessert of s'mores. The party was a big hit and required very little work. The idea of a "toast" party also works well when you want to honor someone's particular accomplishment—guests can "toast" that person all night long!

let party vegan keep you organized

The chapters in this book are organized by type of party or gathering and are divided into two sections. The first section, Anytime Gatherings, includes menus for picnics, potlucks, children's parties, company dinners, and meals with an international theme. In the second section you'll find Holiday Gatherings with menus that follow the calendar from a Super Bowl get-together to a New Year's Eve party, with complete menu strategies and recipes for each event. Many of the recipes can be used interchangeably to suit your needs for different occasions. For example, the Thanksgiving menu is also suitable for Christmas dinner, and the Christmas menu can be adjusted for Easter by substituting seasonal spring produce such as asparagus and new potatoes for the mashed potatoes and spinach with cranberries.

At the beginning of each chapter you'll find a menu, a list of Recipe Swaps, and other tips, followed by the recipes.

The menus in this book reflect a combination of sit-down dinners, buffets, and grazing parties, and many of the recipes are flexible with regard to whether they're served hot, cold, or at room temperature. If a particular dish is best served at a certain temperature, the recipe will specify. In addition, the recipes include make-ahead notes and state if they freeze well and/or can be made in advance. The menus are flexible and can suit your schedule regarding advance preparation. The recipes can be mixed and matched to create dozens of different menus beyond those provided. Wherever possible, I provide time-saving suggestions, including ideas for shortcuts that use store-bought options.

Before you set foot in the kitchen to begin cooking, however, there are a number of things you can do to ensure the fun and stress-free success of your party. It all begins with lists.

Not that anyone needs an excuse to bring a group of friends together, but just in case you prefer to have a reason (any reason) to party, here are some ideas:

TGIF (or Saturday or Sunday)— When there's no work the next day, that's reason enough to celebrate.

A new movie on DVD — It can be even more fun if you make a snack to reflect the theme of the movie, however loose the association: for James Bond, martinis — shaken, not stirred.

Your dog's birthday — Instead of bringing gifts for Fido (who probably already has enough chew toys), ask guests to make a donation to a local animal shelter or other animal welfare charity.

Game night — From board games to charades to a scavenger hunt, this category can also include watching your favorite sport on TV. Sandwiches or other pickup foods are ideal, along with chips and dips.

Awards ceremony — Whether you choose the Tonys, the Oscars, or the Independent Spirit Awards, awards shows are always fun to watch with friends. This party begs for popcorn.

Food or drink tasting — This can be a "formal" tasting, like my chocolate-tasting example. Cookies or wines are also good choices for this kind of party. Or you can host a celebration of a certain seasonal ingredient at its peak, such as strawberries.

Pizza night — Self-explanatory: provide dough, sauce, and toppings. Make together with friends.

The single most important tools for planning, preparing, and hosting any party are a few key lists. They are:

1. Guest List: That initial sheet of paper on which you write the date and time of your party and the names of the guests you plan to invite.

2. Menu and Recipe List: Browse through *Party Vegan* and choose a menu, or make up your own.

3. Shopping Lists: List nonperishables and ingredients for any make-ahead recipes as well as perishables and last minute items.

4. Countdown Timetable: Shows you what needs to be done in the days and weeks leading up to the party.

5. Inventory List: Once you reach this point, you'll want to make a list of food-on-hand and nonfood items you'll need for the party. This involves glancing through your cupboards to count your serving bowls, platters, and utensils so you're not surprised on party day.

Using these lists will help you feel in control of the party from beginning to end and help keep you on track, thus making the entire event as stress-free as possible. The need for lists should seem obvious: once you have it committed to paper, you don't have to be afraid of forgetting something. When I'm in the midst of planning a party, I even keep a tablet and pen at my bedside for those sudden thoughts of inspiration that I might otherwise toss and turn about all night, worried that I'd forget them by the morning.

leading questions for any party

Having a step-by-step plan to guide you through any gathering, from menu planning on through to cleanup, is one of the key elements to a stress-free party. The best place to begin is to first write down the answers to a few basic preliminary questions:

1. What's the occasion? Are you celebrating a special holiday, milestone, or event or do you just feel like throwing a party?

2. When do you want to do it? What time of year? Is there a particular day of the week or time of day that you have in mind?

3. Where will it be held? In most cases the answer to this is "my house or apartment," but you may be planning an outdoor party or one that is held at another location. All these factors will affect the rest of the plans, so it's best to have these details worked out first.

4. How many people are you inviting? Again, the number of people can help dictate what kind of party is practical. For example, if you're only inviting four people, then virtually anything goes in terms of menu and presentation. However, when the numbers go into the double digits, you'll want to be thinking in terms of buffet versus sit-down dinner, or possibly just appetizers and snacks (or desserts) or even a potluck, in which the guests bring the food.

5. How do you plan to invite your guests—by e-mail, phone, or paper invitation? The larger and more special the occasion, the more time you will need to prepare for it. If it's a special birthday celebration, for example, you'll want to send out invitations with RSVPs several weeks in advance so you know how many people to plan for. Obviously, there is much less planning involved if you're just inviting a few friends over for board games and snacks. Whatever the occasion, a countdown timetable can be useful to help ensure things go off without a hitch.

6. What kind of menu do you want? Here you'll decide: Will it be plated or a buffet? Dinner, brunch, or snacks? A cocktail party with hors d'oeuvres or a dessert party with coffee and champagne? The answer to this question is largely dependent on how you respond to the previous questions. The menu and style of the party usually reflects the occasion as well as your lifestyle and how you and your guests would feel the most comfortable.

Once your date is chosen and the guest list is made, it's time to plan the menu. Answering the preliminary questions above have helped you determine the number of guests and whether your menu will be formal or casual, and the quantities of food you will need to prepare the various menu items.

menu planning is a balancing act

When planning a menu, the keyword is "balance," and I have built balance into each menu suggestion in the book. The menu items should have a good balance of textures, such as crunchy, firm, creamy, and so on, as well as temperature: hot, cold, and room temperature. For less last-minute fussing, plan on serving as many room temperature or make-ahead dishes as possible.

There should also be a balance of flavors (spicy, salty, sweet, tart) and the flavors should complement each other, not compete. For example, you generally wouldn't pair distinctly Asian-flavored dishes with Mediterranean ones. Along the same lines, be carefully not to plan for too many similar types of food, whether in texture or ingredient, such as a menu featuring a stuffed tortellini appetizer, a pasta entrée, and a noodle pudding for dessert. (The exception to this would be an ingredient-themed dinner where a special ingredient is the star of the show.)

Color is also key for visual appeal and thought should be given to combining colors that go well together or that evoke a particular mood. For certain holiday-themed parties, specific color combinations (such as orange and black for Halloween) are fun.

A good balance of your time is also important, so keep your menu simple, especially regarding last-minute fussing. If you want to prepare a more complex dish, make sure it's one that can be made ahead. Balance can also apply to the mood and ambience of your party. Let the season and the occasion inspire the menu and ingredients you use for a feeling of harmony and balance.

Once the menu is set, I find it helpful to make a Countdown Timetable in order to keep the details organized and make sure nothing gets overlooked. Here's an idea of how to make one for yourself that can be adapted to see you through any type of event. This guideline is your schedule for shopping and food preparation. You'll need to keep a separate list that includes the date, time, and number of guests you've invited along with the RSVP responses for a final guest count. For a sit-down dinner party or any event including six people or more, you'll want to confirm your RSVPs no later than two weeks prior to the event.

the countdown timetable

Once you have answered the preliminary questions above and planned your menu, it's time to plan the preparation. You will want to move on to your Countdown Timetable and an initial shopping list. It's also a good time to give thought to any help you might need to arrange and to counting your plates, utensils, and serving dishes.

But first things first: begin by making a Countdown Timetable like the one below to use as a step-by-step schedule. When you make your own timetable, be specific about details so you don't forget anything. For example, instead of just jotting down "make guacamole," you should parenthetically add "use the red bowl" and other relevant notes such as "mince tomato for garnish" and "serve with tortilla chips." Once all the details are committed to paper, you'll be amazed at how much more confident you will feel knowing that if you simply check off each item on your list, everything will be taken care of and nothing forgotten.

Obviously, if you're just having a few friends over for snacks and drinks, you don't need to bother with a detailed timetable such as this. However, even a modified version of this timetable can help you stay organized for most parties, whether you're hosting four people or forty.

a countdown timetable

Use the following timetable as a guide to keep yourself organized when throwing a party, large or small. You can customize this timetable and adapt it to your own event and to suit your own style. Write the menu recipe list at the top of your Countdown Timetable, parenthetically noting if you are making double recipes (or more) for any of the menu items.

2 to 3 weeks ahead (longer for larger or more elaborate gatherings):
- List date, number of people, and note other details:
  - Date:
  - Time:

- Number of people: [keep actual guest list on a separate sheet of paper]
- RSVP requested by:

☐ Write up the menu.

☐ Decide on food quantities needed (see page 22) to correspond with the number of guests attending. (You can make adjustments if this number changes.)

☐ Take an inventory of dishes; serving pieces; paper products, including paper towels; aluminum foil; zip-top bags; trash bags; and other items you'll need to buy or borrow for the event.

☐ Read through recipes and make separate lists of what you'll need: groceries (perishable and non-perishable), beverages, dishes, centerpiece, serving pieces, and linens.

☐ Make two shopping lists: the first one listing all nonperishables and ingredients for recipe tests, the second one listing perishables and last-minute items (see next page).

☐ Shop for all the items on your first shopping list (this includes all nonperishable food items, as well as paper products and the ingredients you will need to test any recipes you've never tried before).

☐ Prepare any unfamiliar, time-consuming, or complicated recipes. If the recipes turn out the way you like and if they freeze well, consider freezing what you've prepared to get ahead on the food preparation for the party.

1 to 2 weeks ahead:

☐ Arrange to borrow or rent nonfood items.

☐ Prepare any items in advance that freeze well.

☐ Finalize your inventory of serving pieces and paper products, noting any items that still need to be purchased on your second shopping list.

☐ Gather serving pieces to be used, wash them, and assign the food for them and their placement either by taping small notes to them or by drawing a diagram on paper.

2 to 3 days ahead:

- Review your menu and grocery list; make sure you have everything on hand, including garnishes, beverages, centerpiece, linens, et cetera, and add any last-minute items to the list.
- Do the remainder of your grocery shopping, including perishables.

1 to 2 days ahead:

- Clean your house, leaving only last-minute tidying for the day of the party.
- Defrost any frozen items that you have prepared ahead.
- Set up the tables that will be used for the party.
- Prepare all but the most fragile dishes (such as salads) in advance. If they haven't already been made in advance and frozen, you'll find that most soups, main dishes, dressings, sauces, appetizers, and even desserts can be successfully prepared at least one day ahead of time.

Day of party:

- Do last-minute straightening of the house.
- Finish setting the tables, arranging centerpieces and tableware.
- Set up the coffeemaker and arrange an area for serving coffee.
- Set up the bar area if there will be one.
- Buy ice.
- Chill wine, beer, and other beverages, if needed.
- Place foods in serving bowls and platters and keep perishables refrigerated.
- Arrange any food that needs baking on baking sheets, leaving only final baking, garnishing, and other touches for the last few minutes.

(Note: When you make this list for your own party, it should spell out the specific things that need to be done so that nothing is overlooked.)

1 to 2 hours before:

- Shower and get dressed.
- Take a few minutes to sit down and relax with a cool drink or a cup of coffee or tea.

30 minutes before:

- Put out any foods that don't need refrigeration such as nuts or chips.
- Preheat the oven, if needed.
- Garnish platters or attend to other last-minute details.

15 minutes before:

- By this time, hot foods should be ready to heat (or already heating, for longer-cooking dishes), cold foods cold, and room temperature foods coming to room temperature. (Do not leave heating food unattended unless it is at an extremely low temperature.)
- Take a deep breath and relax for a few minutes before guests arrive.

When guests arrive:

- Offer guests a drink and make them feel welcome.
- If appetizers or nibbles are to be served, you can put them out when you serve drinks. (If you have a spouse, friend, or other person cohosting, ask them to be in charge of drinks.)
- Make sure your guests are introduced to each other.
- When it comes time to serve the food, make an announcement to let people know it's time to dig in.
- At this point, the party is officially launched. Now is the time for you to mingle, talk to your guests, and enjoy yourself.

After the party:

- Put away or discard any food items (discard any perishables that have been at room temperature longer than 2 hours).
- Place dirty dishes in the dishwasher.
- Scrape and soak any dishes that don't fit in the dishwasher.
- Empty any coolers or ice buckets and take out the trash.

As I mentioned previously, you'll need to divide your shopping list into two parts: 1) nonperishables plus ingredients for recipe tests and 2) perishables and last-minute purchases. This allows you to break up the work of shopping and helps you stay organized. You will then be able to prepare some of the recipes in advance to freeze ahead. In addition, purchasing your nonperishables well in advance helps you sharpen the focus of your second shopping list to include the perishable items as well as any last-minute items that you may have forgotten. (See Calculating Food Quantities on page 22.)

Shopping List #1

Includes:

- nonperishable food items
- frozen food items
- beverages
- paper products
- serving pieces or nonperishable centerpiece items
- ingredients needed for test recipes

Shopping List #2

Includes:

- perishable food items
- last-minute items
- perishable centerpiece items

There are two inventory lists you need to make—food and nonfood. The food list will include items that you already have on hand to make the recipes on your menu, such as salt, pepper, or cornstarch. The exception, of course, is if you are low on something or want to have a backup on hand just in case.

The nonfood inventory list includes paper products you need to buy, as well as any decorations or theme-related items, including candles or flowers. It also includes serving pieces (and cookware) that will be needed for every item on your menu. Arrange to buy or borrow or rent anything that you don't have on hand, from chafing dishes to the neighbor's punch bowl.

the "no rules" rules

After decades of planning and preparing parties, both professionally and personally, I have discovered a few things that can help you enjoy yourself at your own party, whether you're cooking for two or two hundred. It boils down to two things: no matter how many tips, guidelines, or ideas you may read about planning the "perfect" party, there really are no rules. The best parties are the ones where you are relaxed, the food and refreshments reflect the occasion and your lifestyle, and everyone is having a good time.

keep it simple

Use the menus, recipes, and ideas in this book as a guide, but always allow yourself the freedom to add your own touches or favorite recipes, or to simply take some shortcuts to simplify the amount of work involved.

Often the most beautiful table and the best-tasting food spring from a "keep it simple" strategy. For example, when fresh tomatoes are in season, instead of hiding chopped tomatoes in a busy, complex, or fussy dish, why not celebrate the tomatoes themselves? What's more beautiful than a large platter of sliced tomatoes of various shapes, sizes, and colors? Drizzled with a vinaigrette, freshly cracked pepper, and a few parsley or basil leaves, the resulting platter is a visual knockout and the taste is sublime.

Certain vegetables and fruits make great containers for dips and crudités as well. Large pumpkins and squash can be used as a tureen for soup, chili, or stew.

"veg to impress"

When I suggest that there are no rules, and you should try to keep things simple, I don't mean that you should set a loaf of bread and a jar of peanut butter on the table and encourage guests to "help themselves" if they get

it'saparty!

hungry. Obviously, you want to prepare delicious food and serve it beauti-fully. That doesn't have to mean silver trays filled with white truffle canapés. There is a middle ground between the extremes of my two examples, which I hope is reflected in the recipes in this book. It's possible to make great vegan food that doesn't cost an arm and a leg to buy or take a staff of cooks to prepare. With simple garnishes, interesting serving pieces, and other flourishes, you can make even simple fare look simply sensational. But remember, guests will be most impressed by warm cheerful hosts who are relaxed and having fun.

less-work-for-you parties

The rewards derived from a successful party in your home are well worth it—that's why we do it—however, there's no way around the fact that having guests over to your home requires time and work. Even if you're merely serving tea and cookies, you still have to clean the house.

My main goal in this book is to provide tips and recipes that make entertain-ing as easy as possible. So, beyond make-ahead recipes and simple menus, there are other ways to entertain that can involve even less work for you.

The most well-known, less-work-for-you party, is the potluck, for which you ask guests to bring the food. Even a potluck involves planning and guidance regarding what everyone brings. If you leave it up to fate, you may end up with twelve bowls of hummus, no chips, and precious little else.

Plan a potluck the same way you plan a party for which you are making all the food. List what you'd like others to bring as kind of a "wish list" of particular dishes, beverages, or other items that are still needed to round out the party. You can then give guests a choice of dishes they can bring. Keep the list up to date as different items are chosen.

Another type of less-work party is one where everyone participates in the cooking at your house. This type of party, in which making the food is the entertainment of the evening, works best for smaller groups. It involves some advance prep on your part, but the actual cooking is done by everyone, so it takes away a lot of the last-minute stress involved in other types of parties.

The kinds of foods that work best for this type of meal include pizza, tacos, sushi, spring rolls, or grilled food on skewers.

In each case, you would need to prepare any toppings or other key elements in advance and set them out for guests to work with. As guests may arrive hungry, and it may be a while before dinner is served, it's a good idea to have some nibbles available so they can munch as they make dinner. Heartier main dishes, such as pizzas or tacos, can "make the meal" while lighter dishes, such as spring rolls, for example, may need an additional item or two, such as a large bowl of fried rice or stir-fried noodles and vegetables, to create a satisfying meal.

mix and match menus

The menus provided in the following chapters are complete; however, I have compiled an additional set of menus (see page 18) that "mix and match" the various recipes to give you more ideas for your upcoming gatherings. While the menu titles suggest particular occasions, the menus and recipes can be used any way you choose for any occasion. For example, if your dinner guests adore Indian food, then you may prefer items from the Indian Feast menu on page 133 rather than either of the Company's Coming menus on pages 18 and 37.

The buffet and appetizer menus include a large variety of recipes, however, you can streamline them to include fewer recipes, depending on the number of people you are entertaining, as well as time and budget factors, or if other people are bringing food items as well.

Another consideration is your own repertoire. If you have particular favorites or tried-and-true dishes that you want to prepare for a particular occasion, you can simply work them into a compatible menu in this book. For example, in that same Company's Coming menu, you could make your special lasagna instead of the Wild Mushroom Ragu over Polenta. The point is that you should feel empowered by these menus, not limited by them. Let them spark your imagination, whether you're planning a casual last-minute gathering or a special dinner party. No rules, just good food and good times—with a minimum of stress.
Here are some "mix-and-match" menu suggestions:

mix-and-match alternate menus

Make-Ahead Holiday Buffet
Antipasto Skewers (page 61)
Very Veggie Lasagna (page 82)
Chilled and Dilled Green Beans
(page 76)
Chocolate-Cherry Cheesecake (page 160)
Strawberries Dipped in Chocolate
(page 71)
Pine Nut–Anise Cookies (page 93)

...

Souper Supper Buffet
Red Bliss Potato and Fennel Soup
(page 155)
Hot and Sour Soup (page 127)
Pea Green Soup (page 163)
Spiced Pita Dippers (page 50)
Spinach-Flecked Chapati (page 136)

...

Sensational Salad Soiree
Romaine and Avocado Salad with
Cilantro-Cumin Vinaigrette (page 194)
Fingerling Potato Salad with Pan-Fried
Arugula Pesto (page 75)
Black Rice Salad (page 226)
Herbed Vegetable Salad (page 219)

...

Casual Grazing Party
Vegetable Dippers with Ranch Dressing
(page 210)
Chickpea-Artichoke Bites with Rosemary
Aïoli (page 153)
Chorizo en Croûte (page 190)
Finger-Lickin' Tempeh Fingers (page 145)
Cherry-Pecan Bars (page 68)
Chocolate Chunk Blondies (page 70)

...

Formal Grazing Party
Spinach Phyllo Cigars with Walnuts and
Figs (page 259)
Artichoke-Stuffed Mushrooms (page 260)
Pastry-Wrapped Stuffed Cherry Peppers
(page 264)
Truffled White Bean Hummus
(page 261)
Fresh Fruit Picks with Two Dips
(page 99)
Pistachio-Dusted Chocolate-Raspberry
Truffles (page 96)

...

Company's Coming, Again
Mixed Greens with Caramelized
Walnuts and Balsamic-Pear Vinaigrette
(page 240)

Two-Potato Shepherd's Pie (page 84)
Sautéed Rainbow Chard with Balsamic
Drizzle (page 159)
Chocolate-Cherry Cheesecake
(page 160)

...

INFORMAL DINNER BUFFET
Chorizo en Croûte (page 190)
Southern Fried Seitan (page 74)
Shamrock Vegetable Salad (page 165)
Antipasto Rice (page xxx)
Mixed Berry Crumble (page 220)

...

A BUNCH FOR BRUNCH
(INFORMAL BUFFET)
Stuffed Dates (page 52)
Mini Blue Corn Pancakes with
Chipotle-Streaked Sour Cream
(page 216)
Tempeh Bacon Triangles (page 202)
Asparagus Quiche-Me-Not (page 200)
Potato Latkes with Cranberry-Apple
Relish (page 252)
Caramel Almond-Oat Bars (page 77)

...

CASUAL LUNCH
Seitan Buffalo Wingz (page 112)
Shamrock Vegetable Salad (page 165)
Three-Potato Salad (page 218)
Ginger-Spice Cupcakes (page 94)

...

CASUAL SPRING DINNER
Teriyaki Shiitake Sticks (page 56)
Caramelized Tofu (page 130)
Coconut Basmati Rice with Cashews
(page 138)
Lemon-Scented Asparagus Bundles
(page 184)
Creamy Lime-Pistachio Parfaits
(page 169)

...

CASUAL AUTUMN DINNER
Mixed Vegetable Curry (page 135)
Brown Rice with Pineapple and Green
Onions (page 129)
Cranberry-Apple Relish (page 235)
Spiced Two-Apple Tart with Cider
Crème (page 246)

...

CASUAL SUMMER DINNER
Polenta Crostini with Eggplant
Tapenade (page 262)
Very Veggie Lasagna (page 82)
Baby Greens with Lemony Vinaigrette
(page 250)
Blueberry-Peach Cobbler (page 213)

...

CASUAL WINTER DINNER
Smoke and Spice Jambalaya (page 174)
Wilted Baby Spinach with
Dried Cranberries (page 245)
Confetti Corn Muffins (page 148)
Chocolate Lover's Brownies (page 92)

how can i help?

If someone offers to help, let them. Just be sure to give specific instructions so things get done the way you want. If you'd rather orchestrate the food yourself, you can simply ask them to see if anything needs refilling, or tell them you don't need help now, but you'd love some help later with cleanup.

cleaning up

Regarding cleanup, some people prefer to leave everything until morning. I think it's much better to get a few things out of the way before calling it a night. Chances are you'll be too keyed up to fall asleep anyway, and you'll feel much better the next day knowing you don't have to face piles of dirty dishes and a huge mess in the kitchen.

At the very least, you should make sure all remaining food is either put away or tossed out. As a food safety measure, be sure to discard any perishable food that has been left out at room temperature for longer than two hours. The trash should be gathered and tied off, preferably taken outside and disposed of. If you don't want to do it all at once, dishes should be rinsed and put in the dishwasher or set aside for hand-washing later. Anything that has food baked-on should be allowed to soak for easy cleanup.

can i bring something?

What if guests ask to bring something? This depends a lot on you, who is asking, how well you know them, and what kind of gathering it is (see page 88 about potlucks). If you're doing all the cooking and you really don't need any additional food, you can simply say you don't need anything. If your party is very theme-specific and your menu is important to you, then you wouldn't want someone showing up with a bowl of his or her favorite salsa, especially if you've worked for weeks on an Asian-themed menu. In such a case it would be best to tell guests you have the food under control but they can bring a beverage (again be specific if a particular type of beverage would work best with your menu). Otherwise, politely decline, telling them that their presence is all that is required.

How much food to make for a party can be tricky, but there are guidelines as well as strategies to help make sure you have enough. When deciding how much food to make, there are several elements to consider:

1. Time of day.

2. Time of year.

3. Number of items on the table. (For example, if you're simply making chili and cornbread, you'll need more chili than if the chili was one of five other dishes on the table.)

4. The type of food being served. Some foods are naturally heavier and more satisfying than others.

5. Type of party and type of guests. A Super Bowl party, for example, will invariably include men with hearty appetites as compared to a baby shower lunch where the guests may be mostly women with (theoretically) lighter appetites. It's also usually true that at a gathering people who know each other well (such as family or close friends) tend to eat more than people who are less well acquainted.

For some general guidelines in estimating how much food you'll need, refer to the Calculating Food Quantities chart on page 22. Keep in mind that estimating food quantities is just that—an estimate—and not an exact science, as there are many factors at work that will impact how much food you need. Many of the recipes in this book serve four to six or six to eight people. Most of the recipes are easily doubled and tripled, as needed.

Plan for more food than you need—you can always freeze the leftovers, enjoy them the next day, or send some home with guests.

Once you've figured out how much food you need, it's time to plan what back-up items to have on hand in case extra people show up, the folks turn out to be extra hungry, or someone drops one of your main dishes on the floor while "helping" you put the food on the table. If you have backup foods on hand, they'll be there if you need them. Check out the Impromptu Party Pantry List on page 23 for a list of such items. If you don't need them you can use them another time, but you'll be glad they were there for the peace of mind they give you, like an insurance policy.

it'saparty!

APPETIZERS AND HORS D'OEUVRES:

■ *For an hors d'oeuvres party.* Plan on serving four to five different items, with at least two of them served hot and the rest served cold or at room temperature. Plan for five pieces total per person for the first hour and four pieces per person for each successive hour.

■ *For a dinner party where an appetizer is served prior to a meal.* Plan on serving only one type of hors d'oeuvre, and allow for no more than two pieces per person. If you're serving a substantial or especially rich main dish (or several courses), be sure to go with something very light as an appetizer, such as a light dip with some crudités or even just a bowl of nuts.

■ *For a lighter meal, a heavier appetizer can balance the meal.* Remember that appetizers served before a meal are not meant to satisfy one's appetite, just to appease it until the main event.

BUFFETS AND SEATED DINNERS:

■ Allow for one serving of each dish per person.

■ For larger groups, make double recipes for main dishes, desserts, and appetizers, but only one and a half that amount for breads, sides, and dips.

■ For buffets, instead of making double or triple amounts of single dishes, you can, instead, increase the number of different dishes you make.

Sometimes, parties just happen without planning, and you have to rely on the contents of your pantry to get you through.

Whenever I need to whip up a satisfying meal using pantry ingredients that can be on the table quickly, I think of three words: pasta, pasta, pasta. Once I put a pot of pasta water on to boil, I sauté some minced garlic and add a large can of diced tomatoes, basil, crushed red pepper, pitted kalamata olives, capers, salt, and pepper. By the time the pasta is cooked, a fragrant and flavorful puttanesca sauce is ready to top it. In the same amount of time, you could make a couscous pilaf or some falafel. Toss a quick salad, and dinner is served.

Here's a list of ingredients to keep on hand in your pantry, freezer, and refrigerator for impromptu entertaining. With the ingredients below, a few stray vegetables, and the usual spices and condiments, you can create quesadillas, ice cream sundaes, chips and dips, tapenade and crostini, rice pilaf, noodles with peanut sauce, a bevy of appetizers (see Puff the Magic Pastry sidebar, page 168), and much more. Keep your pantry stocked with these ingredients and dinner is always just minutes away.

impromptu party pantry list

PANTRY	
salsa	tapenade (in a jar)
vegan chocolate	sun-dried tomatoes
peanut butter	baguettes
tortilla chips and other snacks	corn and flour tortillas

nuts	Asian chili paste
cookies	sriracha sauce
dried pasta	Tabasco sauce
jarred pasta sauce	curry powder or paste
crackers	nori
rice	wasabu
soy sauce	vinegars
unsweetened coconut milk	olive oil
capers	chipotle chiles in adobo
canned beans	canned artichoke hearts
canned diced tomatoes	raspberry or other fruit jam
prepared mustard	canned green chiles
vegan mayonnaise	vegetable broth base
pickled ginger	vegan chocolate chips
sesame seeds	unsweetened cocoa powder

FREEZER

puff pastry	pesto sauce
phyllo dough	pie dough
croutades	pizza dough
vegan ice cream	

REFRIGERATOR

olives	vegan margarine
vegan cream cheese	lemons and limes

recipe subs and swaps

Just as these pantry ingredients can come in handy for an impromptu party, they can also be used during a party in which the best-laid plans have gone awry. Even the best of cooks can have occasional glitches from dropping food on the floor, to burning something if distracted by a phone call. Here are some ways to use on-hand ingredients for simple fixes that can fend off fiascos.

To ensure that your dinner party is stress-free, below are a few important items to keep on hand in case of a culinary emergency. These suggestions can also come in handy as substitutions for particular items, in case you run out of time to prepare everything on the menu. I call them "Last-Minute Rescues" and you'll find these and others listed in various chapters throughout the book where appropriate:

   1. Baguettes: As a backup appetizer, keep a baguette or two on hand to make crostini. A jar of prepared tapenade makes a good topping.
   2. Crackers: If you forget to make your originally planned appetizer and then burn your bread for your backup appetizer of crostini, you'll be really glad you have that extra box of crackers stashed in the cupboard. Pair the crackers with tapenade or a simple dip.
   3. Olive oil and balsamic or sherry vinegar: Keep this dynamic duo on hand for last-minute salad dressing that requires nothing more than a bit of salt and pepper to toss a well-dressed salad.
   4. Bottled marinara sauce and pasta: Keep a jar or two of your favorite bottled marinara sauce on hand, add a splash of wine, and cook up some pasta, and your guests will never know you dropped the previously scheduled lasagna on the floor.
   5. A scoop of vanilla: In the event of a dessert time crunch, keep a quart of vegan vanilla ice cream in the freezer as a backup dessert. Here are a few

ways to transform a simple scoop into a sophisticated and delicious dessert special enough to serve to guests:

- scoop the ice cream into pretty dessert dishes or barware such as martini or wine glasses
- drizzle your favorite liqueur (Grand Marnier, Frangelico, amaretto, Drambuie, or Kahlúa are good choices) on top of each scoop
- garnish with a cookie, piece of fresh fruit, chopped nuts, or other appropriate garnish
- drizzle with some chocolate sauce or other dessert sauce
- make affogato—vanilla ice cream topped with a shot of hot espresso— coffee and ice cream in one dish!

Throughout the book, you will find a variety of helpful tips such as these, variously labeled Recipe Swaps, Last-Minute Rescues, and Go-Withs.

The Recipe Swaps work like this: say you love a particular menu but you find out that one of your guests won't eat mushrooms (which is in the main dish) and another is allergic to chocolate (which is in the dessert). Instead of panicking or ditching the entire menu, simply swap out the recipe in question for one that will make everyone happy. Another way the Recipe Swap can work is when you have a tried-and-true favorite you'd like to prepare instead of one of the recipes in a particular menu.

Following each menu in the book is a list of what I call Go-Withs. This is where I list beverages, breads, or other items that make good accompaniments to the menu. My Go-With lists are by no means cast in stone—feel free to add your own ideas to each menu.

beverage guide: from cocktails to coffee

In planning for beverages at any gathering, it helps if you know what your guests drink. A lot depends on the occasion, too. An outdoor event in the summer will probably translate to more beer, soft drinks, and bottled water. If it's a small dinner party, you'll probably be thinking more in terms of wines.

I recall my parents' parties, where my father mixed drinks to order from a fully stocked bar. Keeping a bar supplied with several varieties of liquor can be expensive and mixing drinks to order can be tedious and time-consuming. Fewer people drink the way they used to, preferring instead to skip serving hard liquor entirely in favor of beer, wine, and soft drinks. Others choose to feature one particular drink, for example margaritas, mojitos, or daiquiris, and incorporate the drink into the theme of the party. Another solution is to serve a punch—it's best to make a nonalcoholic version as well. A punch looks festive, is more economical than a stocked bar, and is easier on you—it simplifies things when you can say "the punch is over there—help yourself." A chilled punch is refreshing in the summer just as warm cider or mulled wine can be a hit in the winter months. Any of these options can simplify the type and amount of liquor needed and you won't need to hire an expert mixologist.

Be sure to set up your bar area away from the food. Usually, the best place for the bar is in the kitchen because of its proximity to a sink and ice. In good weather, you might want to move the bar outside for better traffic flow (especially if your kitchen is small and you need room to work with the food).

When serving beer, especially at casual functions, you can keep bottles or cans of beer chilling in a tub of ice for people to grab as desired. Wine that needs chilling can be kept there as well. Whatever your decision on serving alcohol, be sure to have plenty of nonalcoholic choices available as well, including bottled water, fruit juices, sparkling water, and seltzer. Like chilled beer and wine, these choices can be placed in a tub of ice for guests to serve themselves. Good coffee and a selection of teas are always appreciated, too.

There's no right or wrong choice for serving beverages. In fact, for a larger gathering you can make it a BYOB and take the guesswork out of what everyone wants to drink. (If you do ask people to "bring their own bottle," be sure to provide lots of ice, mixers, glassware, bottled water, and juices.)

For a more formal dinner party, you'll probably want to provide the beverage so that you can match it with the food. While you can certainly offer a choice of cocktails when people arrive, some people don't like to "mix" different kinds of drinks. To that end, I usually like to preface an offer of beverages with something like, "We're having a Pinot Noir with dinner. Would you like to start with

versatile
party punch

A punch is typically made by combining various liquids including fruit juices, tea, and club soda, as well as wines and liquors such as rum or brandy. There are numerous punch permutations available in bartender guides and online. Many families have a punch that they've been making the same way for years. One of my favorites is a versatile punch that I developed simply by increasing the volume of one of my favorite spritzers: a mango-peach and orange juice blend with seltzer water and a squeeze of lime.

For the punch, you combine the same ingredients in a punch bowl (or large clear pitchers, if you don't have a punch bowl) and instead of adding ice, freeze some juice to use instead of ice (so it doesn't dilute the punch). If you substitute champagne or other sparkling white wine for the seltzer, you will have an alcoholic version that is like a cross between a mimosa and a Bellini.

party punch

MAKES 3 QUARTS

Instead of the three different juices, you can substitute two quarts of mango-peach-orange juice blend.

1 quart fresh orange juice
1 pint peach nectar
1 pint mango juice
1 quart seltzer water or sparkling wine
Frozen mango or peach juice cubes
Lime slices, for garnish
Fresh mint leaves, for garnish (optional)

Just before serving, combine all the juices in a punch bowl. Add the seltzer and a few cups of juice cubes. Float the lime slices on top for garnish along with the mint leaves, if using.

that or do you prefer something else?" On other occasions, I've mixed a batch of a particular cocktail in advance to offer guests when they arrive.

Regardless of what other beverages you may or may not be serving, it's a welcome addition to place glasses of water on the table for seated meals. I like to serve water in wine glasses and usually chill a large glass pitcher of water containing lemon slices and some fresh mint or another herb to add a lively yet delicate nuance to the water.

equipment for entertaining

Beyond the usual kitchen appliances, cookware, bakeware, measuring implements, and mixing bowls, there are a number of kitchen tools that come in handy when it's time to make party food. Here's a list of some of the items in my kitchen that I rely on when entertaining:

- pastry cutters (a variety of sizes)
- springform pans (a variety of sizes)
- vegetable peeler
- channel zester
- Microplane grater
- pastry bag with various piping nozzles
- mandoline
- extra baking pans and cookie sheets (for freezing and baking hot hors d'oeuvres, cookies, et cetera)
- slow cookers (great for buffets to keep chili or other hot foods or beverages warm)
- extra plastic storage containers
- zip-top bags (great for storing cut vegetables, marinating ingredients, ground nuts, or crumbs)
- mini muffin tins
- bamboo skewers
- melon baller
- olive pitter

"We eat first with our eyes" is an adage worth remembering when it comes time to plate your food. With a little effort, you can transform just about any food from so-so to sensational. And it doesn't mean you have to spend a lot of money either, although if you do have some nice serving pieces, this would be the time to bring them out of retirement.

Fresh fruits, vegetables, herbs, or edible flowers can be used to garnish platters. Even just a small bunch of grapes can add interest to an hors d'oeuvre tray. Hollowed-out larger produce, such as squashes, melons, bell peppers, pineapples, or cabbages, make great containers for dips. A garnish of fresh herbs can add beauty and fragrance to a plate—just be sure to use ones that don't wilt (e.g., rosemary, thyme, curly parsley). Large (nonpoisonous) leaves make great liners for platters or trays. These include banana leaves, grape leaves, various cabbage leaves, and ornamental kale. Consider using lemon grass stalks or rosemary branches as skewers.

Look for interesting items on which to serve your food, such as wicker baskets, bamboo steamers, mirrors, and so on. Sushi mats can be used to line trays. If serving small bowls of dipping sauces, consider nestling them in a tray filled with dried red or green lentils.

For a buffet, decide how you want to arrange food and then actually set the serving dishes on the table to make sure they fit and the table looks balanced. Once everything is arranged as you like, draw a simple diagram of the arrangement so you can re-create it when the time comes.

The night before the party, begin with an empty dishwasher and clean trash bag. Provide an extra trash receptacle at the bar area if possible. If using candles, make them unscented so they don't compete with food. Choose a color scheme to enhance what you've got in terms of your plates and tablecloths. Use runners, colored cloths, or colored napkins to add contrasting color, and flowers or plants if there's room. For a special seated dinner, use cloth napkins, leaving paper napkins for casual entertaining. For a buffet, consider rolling silverware (or plastic utensils) inside napkins, which can be secured with ribbon and placed in a basket.

Parties intended for mingling work best when the food served doesn't require utensils. I once catered a party where virtually all the food went untouched. We wondered why until we realized the function was a political event and politicians generally don't want to be caught with food in their mouths or unable to freely shake hands. Of course, that's an extreme example, but the point is, when you have a large group of people and you want them to mingle, it's best to serve small bite-size items that can be eaten out of hand.

Whether the food is nibbled, dipped, stuffed, stacked, skewered, wrapped, or rolled, hors d'oeuvres parties are my favorite to prepare and to attend. To me, nothing says "party" like hors d'oeuvres—and most can be made ahead. The food is fun to make and eat. People especially enjoy these kinds of parties since the foods are usually things they don't prepare themselves. Many are economical, too. And because there are no utensils, the cleanup is minimized. Small bites with big flavors also lend themselves to interesting presentations.

If you can get by with no plates (napkins only), then simply arrange platters of hors d'oeuvres on the table, provide napkins, and you're done, although you will need to watch the trays for refills when needed. It's actually best if you can have fresh backup trays/bowls ready so that you can whisk the old one with bits of crumbs and tired garnish off the table, and replace it with a fresh-looking new one, thus keeping your table looking appetizing for the entire event.

For the most aesthetically pleasing arrangements, place each type of hors d'oeuvre on its own tray (no more than two types) with simple garnishes. They should be arranged in odd numbers and in neat diagonal rows without overcrowding. If serving anything with pits, picks, skewers, or shells, provide convenient receptacles to dispose of them. Have extra napkins available as well.

chips, dips, and crudités

If I had to choose one "can't fail" appetizer that's perfect for any gathering, I'd vote for a good dip served with crudités and chips. A dip can be made to complement any type of meal, from guacamole or salsa, to hummus or baba ghanoush. You can make a retro-style onion dip or a creamy "goes with anything" concoction made with fresh herbs. Your presentation can be casual or fancy, depending on the mood you want to set. Best of all, everyone loves to dip and it's easy on you since dips can be made ahead and served when needed with no fuss or bother. Some great dips in this book include:

- Rosemary Aïoli (page 154)
- Artichoke Tapenade (page 38)
- Olive-cado Dip (page 144)
- Rémoulade Sauce (page 173)
- Ranch Dressing (page 210)
- Chipotle-Streaked Sour Cream (page 216)
- Black Olive Tapenade (page 223)
- Five-Story Bean Dip (page 111)
- Smoky Baba Ghanoush (page 49)
- Fava Bean Hummus (page 48)

For chips, you can make your own potato chips, tortilla chips, or pita chips (try the Spiced Pita Dippers on page 50), or simply buy a few bags of your favorites at the store.

For an interesting presentation for crudités, go vertical instead of horizontal. Simply arrange vegetables standing up in glasses or cups and nestle them in a basket or other interesting container, varying the vegetables with different heights. The colors of the vegetables can be used for dramatic appeal, whether you choose a monochromatic palette, or two or more colors. Your arrangement can include just one or two types of vegetables, or several. With crudités, almost anything goes.

For an arrangement that looks like it was plucked from nature, serve your dip in a hollowed-out vegetable, nestle it among the crudités, and garnish with chive blossoms, purple frilly kale, or edible flowers. You can choose one favorite vegetable, or three or more, depending on how many people you're serving and how much advance cutting you want to do. If serving only one vegetable, be sure to garnish the platter with something to add a complementary but contrasting color for visual appeal. For one party, I arranged lightly steamed asparagus in a clear vase and tied a purple ribbon around the vase. Next to it was a bowl of lemony dip garnished with edible purple flowers. The effect was beautiful.

Here's a list of my favorite veggies to consider for dipping:

- Asparagus (lightly blanched)
- Belgian endive
- Celery
- Carrots
- Broccoli (very lightly blanched)
- Cauliflower
- Cherry or grape tomatoes
- Cucumber (English)
- Baby bok choy
- Fennel
- Bell peppers
- Zucchini and yellow squash
- Radishes
- Snow peas or snap peas (very lightly blanched)
- Jicama

anytime
gatherings

a dinner party

When company's coming, you want a menu you can count on that is easy to prepare and guaranteed to taste great. I especially like recipes that can be assembled in advance to minimize the time spent in the kitchen after guests arrive. The kitchen stays neater that way, too.

As discussed in the previous chapter, the more organized you are and the more preparation you do in advance, the more you will be able to enjoy your own get-together. This is especially true if you're planning a sit-down dinner party.

For this type of occasion, I've gone with an Italian menu, but with a twist. The various elements are all Italian, but they are served in unexpected ways. For example, the biscotti are served as an appetizer. Normally sweet and eaten after dinner with coffee, these biscotti are made savory with sun-dried tomatoes and olives. They are enjoyed with an Artichoke Tapenade, which is usually spread on crackers or crostini. Both the tapenade and biscotti can be made a day ahead.

The first course is a sophisticated salad made with radicchio and butterhead lettuce dressed with an assertive walnut-pesto dressing. If you make the dressing the day before, and wash the lettuce earlier in the day, all that remains is to plate and serve at mealtime.

The main dish, a flavorful mushroom ragu, is a make-ahead marvel, too, tasting even better after its flavors have a chance to meld. The polenta, a nice change from the usual pasta, is made in advance and then chilled and sliced before a quick trip into the oven before serving. Some warm garlic bread makes a welcome accompaniment.

Continuing the Italian with a twist theme, the dessert is an updated version of an old favorite, tiramisù, this time made with chocolate cake and Grand Marnier for a decadent finish.

the menu

COMPANY'S COMING | Italian with a Twist

Artichoke Tapenade
Sun-Dried Tomato and Green Olive Biscotti
Butterhead and Radicchio Salad with
   Walnut-Pesto Dressing
Wild Mushroom Ragu over Polenta
Orange-Kissed Chocolate Tiramisù

Go-Withs: *warm garlic bread; wine, coffee or tea*

recipe swaps

Appetizer: *Pastry-Wrapped Stuffed Cherry Peppers
   (page 264)*

Salad: *Baby Greens with Lemony Vinaigrette (page 250)*

Main Dish: *Very Veggie Lasagna (page 82) or
   Roasted Eggplant and Potato Torta (page 182)*

Dessert: *Spiced Two-Apple Tart with Cider Crème (page
   246) or Chocolate "Pots de Crème" (page 204)*

artichoke tapenade

MAKE ABOUT 2 CUPS

This luscious tapenade swaps out artichokes for olives, but the requisite capers remain, along with a squeeze of lemon to brighten the flavor. Serve with the biscotti (facing page) or as a topping for crostini or bruschetta.

1 (9-ounce) package frozen artichoke hearts or 1 (14-ounce) can unmarinated artichoke hearts

¼ cup capers, drained

1 teaspoon fresh lemon juice

Pinch dried marjoram

¼ teaspoon salt

⅛ teaspoon freshly ground black pepper

3 tablespoons olive oil

1. If using frozen artichoke hearts, cook them according to package directions. Drain well and cool. If using canned artichokes, drain them well.

2. In a food processor combine the artichokes and capers and pulse until finely chopped. Add the juice, marjoram, salt, and pepper. Pour in the oil and blend to a smooth paste.

3. Use a rubber spatula to scrape the tapenade into a small bowl. If not using right away, cover and refrigerate until needed. Properly stored, it will keep for up to 5 days.

last-minute rescues

Keep some baguettes on hand on the off chance something unforeseen happens to your biscotti. This way, you'll be able to make crostini instead. Have a jar of prepared tapenade on hand, as well, in case you need it.

Keep a jar or two of bottled marinara sauce on hand as a backup sauce. Just add a splash of wine and some herbs and move forward with dinner.

The emergency dessert rescue for any party is a stash of vegan ice cream in the freezer. Endlessly versatile, it can be topped with chocolate, fruit, or nuts and no one will know you didn't have time to make a dessert.

sun-dried tomato and green olive biscotti

Crisp and crunchy biscotti are too delicious to reserve for dessert alone. In this recipe olive- and pine nut–studded biscotti take a savory turn as an appetizer. They are paired here with Artichoke Tapenade, but are great on their own as well.

1½ cups all-purpose flour
2 teaspoons baking powder
½ teaspoon sugar
½ teaspoon salt
⅛ teaspoon freshly ground black
 pepper
1 teaspoon ground fennel seed

½ cup water
3 tablespoons olive oil
⅓ cup chopped pitted green olives
⅓ cup minced oil-packed sun-
 dried tomatoes
⅓ cup crushed pine nuts
 (optional)

1. Preheat the oven to 350°F. Lightly grease a baking sheet and set aside. In a large bowl, combine the flour, baking powder, sugar, salt, pepper, and fennel seed. Add the water, oil, olives, tomatoes, and pine nuts, if using, and mix to form a cohesive dough. Refrigerate the dough for 10 minutes.

2. Divide the dough in half and shape each half into a 4 x 6-inch loaf, about 1 inch thick. Place the loaves on the prepared baking sheet. Bake until golden and a toothpick inserted in the center comes out clean, about 25 minutes. Remove from the oven and cool for 10 minutes on wire rack. Reduce the oven temperature to 275°F.

3. Use a serrated knife to cut each loaf into ½-inch-thick slices. Place the sliced biscotti on their side on an ungreased baking sheet and bake for 10 minutes, then flip the biscotti and bake 10 minutes longer. Cool completely on a wire rack before storing in an airtight container where they will keep for several days.

make ahead   **quick & easy**

butterhead and radicchio salad with walnut-pesto dressing

MAKES 4 SERVINGS

Soft and sweet butterhead lettuce and slightly bitter radicchio join forces in this lush and lovely salad festooned with olives, tomatoes, and walnuts. A rich and flavorful walnut-pesto dressing brings it all together.

2 garlic cloves, crushed

¼ cup raw walnut pieces

½ cup fresh basil or parsley

1½ tablespoons fresh lemon juice

½ teaspoon sugar

½ teaspoon salt

Freshly ground black pepper

¼ cup walnut or olive oil

¼ cup plain unsweetened soy milk or other nondairy milk

3 cups torn butterhead lettuce leaves

2 cups chopped radicchio

8 kalamata olives, pitted

8 cherry or grape tomatoes, halved lengthwise

1. In a blender or food processor, combine the garlic and walnuts and process until finely ground. Add the basil, juice, sugar, salt, and several grindings of black pepper and process to a paste. Add the oil and soy milk and process until smooth and well blended. Taste and adjust the seasonings, if necessary. Transfer to a small bowl and set aside or cover and refrigerate until needed.

2. When ready to serve, combine the lettuce and radicchio in a large bowl. Add the olives and tomatoes. Drizzle with the dressing and toss gently to coat. Serve immediately.

40

make ahead   **quick & easy**

wild mushroom ragu over polenta

Crisp slices of golden polenta blanketed with a zesty tomato ragu made opulent with wild mushrooms and kalamata olives, is ideal company fare since the components can be made ahead of time to eliminate last-minute fussing.

Variations: For a touch of creative whimsy, instead of spreading the polenta in a loaf pan and cutting into slices, you can spread the polenta evenly on a rimmed baking sheet and chill. Once the polenta is chilled, you can then use a cookie or canapé cutter of your choice to cut the polenta into different shapes. If you don't have cutters, you can use a juice glass to cut the polenta into circles. You can also cut the slices of polenta made in the loaf pan on the diagonal to create triangles or cut the slices into bars.

POLENTA
5 cups water
½ teaspoon salt
1½ cups cornmeal polenta

RAGU
1 tablespoon olive oil
1 medium yellow onion,
   coarsely chopped
3 garlic cloves, coarsely chopped
8 ounces mixed mushrooms,
   such as cremini and porcini,
   lightly rinsed, patted dry, and
   cut into ½-inch slices

1 (14.5-ounce) can crushed
   tomatoes
1 (14.5-ounce) can diced
   tomatoes, drained
1 teaspoon dried basil
½ teaspoon dried marjoram
½ teaspoon ground fennel seed
¼ teaspoon crushed red pepper
Salt and freshly ground black
   pepper
½ cup kalamata olives, pitted
   and halved

1. Make the polenta: Lightly grease a 9-inch loaf pan and set aside. In a large pot, bring the water to boil over high heat. Add the salt and slowly stream in the polenta, whisking constantly. Reduce the heat to medium-low and continue whisking until the polenta pulls away from the sides of the pot, about 20 minutes.

2. Smooth the polenta evenly into the prepared loaf pan and refrigerate until chilled and firm, about 2 hours.

3. Make the ragu: In a medium saucepan, heat the oil over medium heat. Add the onion, cover, and cook until softened, about 5 minutes. Add the garlic and mushrooms and cook until softened, about 3 minutes.

4. Stir in the crushed tomatoes, diced tomatoes, basil, marjoram, fennel seed, and red pepper. Season with salt and black pepper, to taste. Reduce the heat to low and simmer for 20 minutes. Stir in the olives. If making ahead, cool completely then refrigerate until needed. Tightly covered, the ragu will keep well in the refrigerator for up to 3 days. If serving right away, keep warm while you finish preparing the polenta.

5. Preheat the oven to 375°F. Lightly grease a baking sheet and set aside. Remove the firm polenta from the refrigerator and turn it out of the pan onto a cutting board. Cut the polenta into ½-inch slices. Place the sliced polenta on the prepared baking sheet. Brush with more oil and season with salt and black pepper, to taste. Bake until hot, turning once about halfway through, about 20 minutes total.

6. When ready to serve, arrange a portion of the polenta in the center of each dinner plate and top with a large spoonful of the mushroom ragu. Serve hot.

make ahead   **quick & easy**

orange-kissed chocolate tiramisù

Tiramisù gets a sophisticated update with a chocolate base complemented by the flavor of orange. The Grand Marnier–laced crème layer, made with cashew butter and vegan cream cheese, is so delicious, you'll want to eat it on the spot, but try to save some for the tiramisù.

CAKE

1 cup plain or vanilla soy milk or other nondairy milk

1 teaspoon apple cider vinegar

2 tablespoons vegan margarine

⅔ cup sugar

2 tablespoons neutral vegetable oil

1 teaspoon pure vanilla extract

1½ cups all-purpose flour

½ cup unsweetened cocoa powder

1 teaspoon baking powder

½ teaspoon baking soda

¼ teaspoon salt

SYRUP

½ cup water

¼ cup sugar

⅓ cup Grand Marnier

CRÈME

1 cup cashew butter

1 cup vegan cream cheese

½ cup sugar

⅓ cup plain or vanilla soy milk or other nondairy milk

2 tablespoons Grand Marnier

1 teaspoon pure vanilla extract

1 teaspoon orange extract

GARNISH

1 teaspoon ground dried candied orange peel

Candied orange peel (optional)

Chocolate curls (optional)

1. Make the cake: Preheat the oven to 350°F. Lightly grease an 8-inch square baking pan and set aside.

2. In a small bowl, combine the soy milk and vinegar and set aside. In a large bowl, combine the margarine and sugar and cream together with an electric mixer on medium speed. Add the oil and vanilla and scrape down the sides, mixing well. Add the soy milk mixture and mix well.

3. In a separate large bowl, combine the flour, cocoa, baking powder, baking soda, and salt. Mix well to combine. Add the dry mixture to the wet

adinner**party**

mixture, about one-third at a time, mixing with the electric mixer on medium speed after each addition until just combined. Do not overmix. Scrape the batter into the prepared pan and bake until a toothpick inserted in the center comes out clean, about 30 minutes. Set aside to cool completely in the pan on a wire rack.

4. Make the syrup: In a small saucepan, bring the water to boil over high heat. Add the sugar and cook, stirring, until the sugar is dissolved, about 2 minutes. Remove from the heat and stir in the Grand Marnier. Set aside to cool.

5. Make the crème: In a food processor, combine the cashew butter, cream cheese, sugar, soy milk, Grand Marnier, and the vanilla and orange extracts. Process until well blended and smooth and creamy.

6. Turn the cake out of the pan onto a flat work surface. Use a serrated knife to cut the cake in half horizontally, to make 2 layers. Arrange 1 layer of the cake (whether in a single large piece or 4 smaller pieces) back into the same cake pan and brush the cake with half of the syrup.

7. Spread half of the crème mixture on top of the cake, then place the remaining cake layer on top. Brush the remaining syrup onto the second cake layer and spread the remaining crème on top. Cover and refrigerate for at least 2 hours or up to 10 hours.

8. When ready to serve, garnish with a dusting of powdered orange peel and pieces of candied orange peel or chocolate curls, if using.

make ahead   **quick & easy**

crowd
control

Each of the menus in this chapter consists of a different theme and the recipes work well at both casual and fancy gatherings. You can make them all for a very large party and arrange them at separate "stations" or prepare just one or more for smaller get-togethers. In deciding how many stations to set up, you'll also want to consider how much space you have to arrange the food and how much help you have to set it all up.

The recipes in this chapter can be prepared well ahead of time (but allow for last-minute reheating for hot items). Best of all, they are pickup foods, meaning you can eat them without utensils.

menus
stations everyone!

MOROCCAN STATION

Fava Bean Hummus
Smoky Baba Ghanoush
Spiced Pita Dippers
Mini Falafel
Stuffed Dates

Go-Withs: *olives, dried apricots, mini pita breads, root vegetable crisps*

JAPANESE STATION

Edamame
Japanese Pancakes (Okonomiyaki)
Teriyaki Shiitake Sticks
Sushi Rice Balls
Gingered "Crab" Cups with Wasabi Cream Cheese

Go-Withs: *rice crackers, wasabi peas*

ANTIPASTO STATION

Antipasto Skewers
Mini Focaccia with Tapenade
Zucchini Cups with Tomato Concassé
Arugula and White Bean Crostini
Pesto-Stuffed Baby Potatoes

Go-Withs: *marinated mushrooms, olives, breadsticks*

DESSERT STATION

Coconut Snowballs
Cherry-Pecan Bars
Italian Wedding Cookies
Chocolate Chunk Blondies
Strawberries Dipped in Chocolate

Go-Withs: *bakery wedding cake (for a wedding reception), bakery breads; champagne punch*

moroccan station

fava bean hummus

Similar to chickpea hummus, this Moroccan dip made with fava beans (and no tahini) is called *bessara*. Traditionally it is served warm, but tastes fine at room temperature, too. If favas are unavailable, substitute cooked chickpeas or other cooked beans. Serve with the Spiced Pita Dippers (page 50), along with sliced raw vegetables, or crackers.

2 to 3 garlic cloves
½ teaspoon salt
1½ cups cooked fava beans
2 tablespoons fresh lemon juice
¼ teaspoon ground cumin
¼ teaspoon sweet paprika

⅛ teaspoon ground cayenne
3 tablespoons olive oil
2 tablespoons minced fresh parsley
⅓ cup finely chopped pitted Moroccan olives

1. In a food processor, combine the garlic and salt and process until finely minced. Add the fava beans, lemon juice, cumin, paprika, and cayenne, and process until well blended.

2. With the machine running, stream in the oil and process until smooth and creamy. Transfer to a medium bowl and sprinkle the parsley on top, around the outer perimeter of the hummus. Sprinkle the olives in a circle inside the circle of parsley. If not using right away, cover and refrigerate until needed. Properly stored, this will keep for up to 3 days.

smoky baba ghanoush

The creamy eggplant dip known as baba ghanoush is given added depth of flavor by roasting the eggplants and adding a touch of liquid smoke and smoked paprika.

2 small eggplants, halved lengthwise
2 garlic cloves, slivered
¼ cup tahini (sesame paste)
2 tablespoons fresh lemon juice

¼ teaspoon liquid smoke
½ teaspoon salt
¼ teaspoon smoked paprika
2 tablespoons fresh parsley

1. Preheat the oven to 425°F. Lightly oil a 9 x 13-inch baking pan and set aside. Make small slits in the cut sides of the eggplants and press the garlic slivers into them. Transfer the eggplant halves, cut side down, to the prepared baking pan and bake until soft, 25 to 30 minutes. Set aside to cool.

2. Scoop the cooked eggplant flesh into a food processor. Add the tahini, lemon juice, liquid smoke, and salt, and process until smooth. Taste and adjust the seasonings, if necessary.

3. Transfer to a medium bowl and sprinkle with the paprika. Sprinkle the parsley around the perimeter to frame the baba ghanoush. Serve at room temperature. If not using right away, cover and refrigerate until needed. Properly stored, this will keep for up to 3 days.

make ahead   **quick & easy**

spiced pita dippers

These little dippers have a fresh flavor you won't find in store-bought pita chips. Best of all, you can customize the flavor to suit your own tastes—make some spicier and some on the mild side.

4 (7-inch) pita breads
Olive oil
Smoked paprika
Ground cumin

Ground coriander
Ground cayenne
Salt

1. Preheat the oven to 350°F. Carefully slice each pita bread into two circles with a serrated knife. Lightly brush the oil onto the inner side of each circle.

2. Cut the pita circles into eighths and arrange the pieces on an ungreased baking sheet in a single layer, oil side up. Sprinkle with the spices and salt, to taste. Bake until golden brown, about 10 minutes. Serve at room temperature. These are best eaten on the day they are made. Store at room temperature.

Hosting a large get-together is a significant undertaking, whether it's something as special as a wedding reception or just a casual open house. The good news is that there are ways to simplify cooking for a crowd so that it doesn't have to be a major production. The way I do this is to set up several food "stations" with different types of dishes. This allows guests to pick and choose what they want and it adds to the excitement of the party.

The number of stations and the amount of food they contain will depend on your space and the number of guests. With pickup food set out on different tables, guests can mingle and graze throughout the party. This setup is much easier on you than providing a seated meal or even a buffet menu that requires a knife and fork.

mini falafel

When you make a scaled-down version of the classic chickpea patties known as falafel, you end up with a tasty pickup food that makes a great addition to any party menu. These are especially good enlivened with a dab of harissa mayo.

1½ cups cooked or 1 (15.5-ounce) can chickpeas, drained and rinsed
1 small yellow onion, coarsely chopped
3 garlic cloves, coarsely chopped
¼ cup coarsely chopped fresh parsley

⅓ cup chickpea flour
1 teaspoon ground cumin
½ teaspoon ground coriander
¾ teaspoon salt
⅛ teaspoon freshly ground black pepper
Olive oil, for frying
Harissa mayo (see note below)

1. In a food processor, combine the chickpeas, onion, garlic, parsley, chickpea flour, cumin, coriander, salt, and pepper and process to combine. Refrigerate for 20 minutes.

2. Form the mixture into small balls, about 1 inch in diameter. If the mixture is not firm enough, add up to ¼ cup more flour, a little at a time, until the desired consistency is reached. Flatten the balls into patties.

3. In a large skillet, heat a thin layer of oil over medium-high heat. Add the falafel and cook, turning once, until golden brown, about 8 minutes total. Arrange on a platter. Serve with harissa mayo. If not serving right away, bring the falafel to room temperature and store tightly covered in the refrigerator where they will keep for several days or frozen for up to 2 weeks.

Note: To make harissa mayo, combine ½ cup vegan mayo and 1 to 2 tablespoons harissa in a small bowl and stir well to blend.

make ahead   **quick & easy**

stuffed dates

No Moroccan table is complete without dates and these stuffed dates are all dressed up for a party. In addition to being filled with whole roasted almonds, the dates are topped with a dab of almond butter and sprinkled with orange zest.

24 whole pitted dates
¼ cup almond butter
24 whole roasted almonds

1 tablespoon finely grated
   orange zest

1. Cut a slit lengthwise in each date and set aside.

2. Place the almond butter in a pastry bag with a small tip or in a zip-top bag with one of the bottom corners snipped off. Pipe a very small dot of almond butter into each of the dates.

3. Place an almond inside each date on top of the almond butter, allowing a portion of the almond to protrude from the date. Pipe a very small dot of almond butter on top of each of the almonds and top each with a small amount of zest. Arrange on a platter to serve.

make ahead   **quick & easy**

japanese station

edamame

Edamame make a fun, healthful, tasty addition to any gathering. These green soybeans in the pod are available in well-stocked supermarkets, natural food stores, and Asian markets and are sold both fresh and frozen.

1 pound fresh or frozen
  edamame in the pod

Coarse salt

1. Steam the edamame until tender, 5 to 7 minutes. Rinse under cold water, then drain well and pat dry.

2. Transfer to a bowl and season with salt. If not using right away, cover and refrigerate for up to 2 days.

japanese pancakes (okonomiyaki)

These are usually made in a large round resembling a pizza and cut into wedges. This recipe scales down this tasty treat to small pancakes for pickup food at a party. Traditional *okonomiyaki* contain the somewhat gelatinous pureed mountain yam that helps hold the pancake together. Since it may be difficult to find, this recipe uses tapioca flour instead with good results.

⅓ cup vegan mayonnaise
½ teaspoon sriracha sauce
¾ cup all-purpose flour
¼ cup tapioca flour
2 cups finely shredded napa
  cabbage, blotted dry
2 green onions, minced

2 tablespoons nori flakes or
  finely slivered nori
1 tablespoon nutritional yeast
1 tablespoon tamari soy sauce
¼ teaspoon liquid smoke
⅔ cup vegetable broth
Neutral vegetable oil, for frying

1. In a small bowl, combine the mayonnaise and sriracha, stirring to blend well. Set aside.

2. In a large bowl, combine both flours, the cabbage, green onions, and nori. Stir in the yeast, tamari, liquid smoke, and broth, and mix well to combine.

3. In a large skillet, heat a thin layer of oil over medium heat. Spoon about 1½ tablespoons of the pancake mixture into the hot skillet, pressing with a metal spatula to flatten. Repeat with additional mixture, making as many pancakes as will fit in the skillet without crowding. Cook until golden brown on both sides, 6 to 7 minutes per side.

4. Transfer to a platter and keep warm while you make the rest of the pancakes. To serve, top each pancake with a small amount of the sriracha mayonnaise. If not using right away, bring the pancakes to room temperature, then cover and refrigerate for up to 2 days.

make ahead   **quick & easy**

crowdcontrol

teriyaki shiitake sticks

Cute, colorful, and loaded with flavor, shiitake mushrooms and snow peas are threaded onto picks or skewers for a fun and easy pickup appetizer.

1/3 cup soy sauce

1/4 cup mirin

3 tablespoons fresh orange juice

3 tablespoons sugar

1 teaspoon grated fresh ginger

1 teaspoon cornstarch dissolved in 2 tablespoons water

24 small shiitake mushroom caps, lightly rinsed and patted dry

24 large snow peas, trimmed and blanched

1. Soak sturdy toothpicks or bamboo skewers in water for 30 minutes.

2. In a medium saucepan, combine the soy sauce, mirin, juice, sugar, and ginger and bring to a boil over high heat. Reduce heat to medium and simmer until syrupy, about 10 minutes. Stir in the cornstarch mixture and stir until thickened. Add the mushrooms to the sauce and toss to coat. Simmer 5 minutes longer, then set aside at room temperature for 30 minutes to marinate. Preheat the oven to 400°F.

3. Remove the mushrooms from the marinade; set the marinade aside. Wrap each snow pea around a mushroom and thread onto the soaked toothpicks or skewers. If using toothpicks, one mushroom per pick is sufficient; if using skewers, you may add a second mushroom.

4. Arrange the shiitake sticks on a baking sheet and drizzle with the reserved marinade. Bake until the mushrooms are tender, about 10 minutes. These can be assembled and refrigerated up to a day ahead of time prior to baking and serving.

sushi rice balls

These little rice balls contain the flavors of sushi with a fraction of the fuss. They should be made ahead and refrigerated and can be served chilled or at room temperature.

1 cup short-grain sushi rice
1 cup water
½ cup rice vinegar
¼ cup sugar
¼ cup pickled ginger, cut into 24 ¼ x ½-inch strips

1 sheet nori, cut into 24 ¼ x ½-inch strips
1 teaspoon wasabi paste

1. Place the rice in a large bowl and add enough cold water to cover. Stir the rice until the water turns cloudy, then pour off the water and repeat once or twice with fresh water until the water is almost clear.

2. Drain the rice and place in a medium saucepan. Add the 1 cup water, cover, and bring to a boil over high heat, then reduce the heat to medium and simmer until the water is absorbed and the rice is tender, about 15 minutes. Remove from the heat and let stand, covered, for 5 minutes.

3. In a small saucepan, combine the vinegar and sugar and bring to a boil, stirring, until the sugar dissolves. Remove from the heat to cool.

4. Spread the cooked rice in a large shallow baking pan and drizzle with the vinegar mixture, tossing gently to combine. Cool the rice to room temperature, tossing the rice gently to cool. Divide the rice into 24 equal portions, using dampened fingers to shape the portions into tight balls.

5. Arrange one strip each of the ginger and nori on top of each rice ball, pressing the ginger and nori into the rice so they adhere to it.

6. Garnish the tops of some or all of the sushi balls with a tiny dab of wasabi. Serve chilled or at room temperature. If not using right away, cover tightly and refrigerate for up to a day.

make ahead   **quick & easy**

gingered "crab" cups with wasabi cream cheese

MAKES ABOUT 36 "CRAB" CUPS

Diminutive golden brown "crab" balls are nestled in crunchy phyllo cups and topped with wasabi cream cheese for a sensational blending of textures and flavors. To save time, make the phyllo cups ahead or buy them readymade in the freezer case of your supermarket. The "crab" balls and topping can be made ahead, too, for another appetizer that requires only a last minute reheat before serving.

4 ounces phyllo dough

2 tablespoons vegan margarine, melted

8 ounces extra-firm tofu, drained and crumbled

1 celery rib, minced

¼ cup minced yellow onion

½ cup panko bread crumbs

¼ cup vegan mayonnaise

2 tablespoons fresh lemon juice

1 tablespoon kelp flakes

1½ teaspoons grated fresh ginger

½ teaspoon Old Bay seasoning

½ teaspoon salt

¼ teaspoon freshly ground black pepper

½ cup vegan cream cheese, at room temperature

1 teaspoon wasabi paste

Plain unsweetened soy milk or other nondairy milk, if needed

Cilantro leaves, for garnish

1. Preheat the oven to 350°F. Lightly grease 2 mini muffin tins and set aside.

2. Brush 1 sheet of phyllo with the melted margarine. Use a sharp knife to cut it into 2-inch squares. Line each muffin cup with 4 phyllo squares. Place each square at slightly different angles. Repeat until all the pastry has been used.

3. Bake until the cups are golden brown, about 6 minutes. Carefully remove the phyllo cups from the muffin pan and let them cool on a wire rack.

4. In a large bowl, combine the tofu, celery, onion, panko, mayonnaise, juice, kelp, ginger, Old Bay seasoning, salt, and pepper. Mix together until well combined.

5. Use a teaspoon to portion out the mixture into small 1 to 1½-inch cakes. Use your hands to shape them into round cakes and place them onto a parchment-lined baking sheet. Bake until golden brown, about 30 minutes.

6. In a small bowl, blend together the cream cheese and the wasabi, adding a splash of soy milk if needed to make a smooth but thick topping.

7. To serve, place a "crab" ball into each phyllo cup, garnish with a small dot of wasabi cream cheese piped on with a pastry bag or a zip-top bag with a tiny piece of a bottom corner snipped off. Add a cilantro leaf to each and arrange them on a platter. Serve at room temperature. The components can all be made ahead of time and then assembled when ready to serve.

make ahead   **quick & easy**

antipasto
station

antipasto skewers

MAKES 24 SKEWERS

All our favorite tidbits from an antipasto platter—on one easy-to-eat skewer. You will need 24 bamboo skewers for this recipe—the 6-inch ones work great.

1 garlic clove, crushed

3 tablespoons olive oil

1½ tablespoons white wine vinegar

½ teaspoon sugar

¼ teaspoon salt

¼ teaspoon freshly ground black pepper

1 tablespoon minced fresh parsley

1 teaspoon minced fresh basil or ½ teaspoon dried

½ teaspoon minced fresh oregano or ¼ teaspoon dried

12 small white mushrooms, lightly rinsed, patted dry, and halved

24 pitted kalamata olives

24 cooked medium pasta shells (about 1-inch diameter)

12 small cherry tomatoes, halved

6 small canned or cooked frozen artichoke hearts, quartered

1. In a shallow bowl, combine the garlic, oil, vinegar, sugar, salt, pepper, parsley, basil, and oregano, stirring to blend. Add the mushrooms and toss to coat. Cover and set aside at room temperature to marinate for 30 minutes.

2. Onto each skewer thread 1 mushroom half, 1 olive, 1 pasta shell, 1 cherry tomato half, and 1 artichoke heart piece. Repeat with the remaining ingredients on the remaining skewers.

3. Arrange on a platter and drizzle with the remaining marinade. Serve at room temperature. If not using right away, cover and refrigerate for up to a day.

make ahead   **quick & easy**

crowdcontrol

mini focaccia with tapenade

These hearty and flavorful appetizers taste best served warm or at room temperature. They can be made ahead of time and then quickly reheated when ready to serve.

2 cups bread flour
2¼ teaspoons active dry yeast
1 teaspoon salt
2 teaspoons olive oil
1 cup warm water
1 garlic clove
1 cup pitted kalamata olives
2 tablespoons capers, drained

2 teaspoons fresh lemon juice
⅛ teaspoon freshly ground black pepper
Finely minced tomato, small basil leaves, and small rosemary sprigs, for garnish

1. In a large bowl, combine the flour, yeast, and salt. Stir in 1 teaspoon of the oil and as much of the water as needed to make a cohesive dough. Mix until combined then use your hands to knead it until it holds together.

2. Transfer the dough to a floured work surface and knead until it is smooth and elastic, about 10 minutes. Shape the dough into a smooth ball and place in an oiled bowl. Cover with plastic wrap and let rise at room temperature in a warm spot for 1 hour.

3. In a food processor, mince the garlic. Add the olives, capers, juice, the remaining 1 teaspoon oil, and the pepper and process to a coarse paste. Transfer to a small bowl and set aside.

4. Preheat the oven to 400°F. After the dough has risen, transfer it to a floured work surface, punch it down, and gently stretch and roll it to ¼-inch thickness. Use a 2-inch pastry cutter or drinking glass to cut out 24 rounds. Place them on an ungreased baking sheet and bake until crisp and golden brown, about 15 minutes. While still warm, top each round with a teaspoon of tapenade. Sprinkle with a few bits of minced tomato, others with a basil leaf, and the rest with rosemary sprigs. Arrange on a platter and serve warm. If not using right away, leave off the garnishes until ready to serve and cover the foccacia and store at room temperature for up to several hours, reheating briefly just before garnishing and serving.

zucchini cups with tomato concassé

MAKES ABOUT 24 CUPS

Pretty to look at and delicious to eat, these zucchini cups are made ahead and can be served chilled or at room temperature.

4 to 5 small zucchini, ends trimmed

6 to 8 ripe Roma tomatoes

1 tablespoon olive oil

2 tablespoons minced fresh parsley

Salt and freshly ground black pepper

Whole parsley or basil leaves, for garnish

1. Cut the zucchini into 1-inch pieces with flat bottoms so they stand up. Use a small spoon or melon baller to scoop out some of the center of each piece of zucchini to form little cups. Blanch the zucchini cups in a saucepan of boiling salted water to soften slightly, about 1 minute. Drain, run under cold water to stop the cooking process, and drain again. Arrange the zucchini on paper towels, cup side down, and set aside.

2. Cut an X in the bottom of the tomatoes and immerse them in a saucepan of boiling water to loosen the skin, about 30 seconds. Remove the tomatoes from the water and submerge them in a bowl of ice water. Peel the skin from the tomatoes, then cut them in wedges and remove the seeds.

3. Coarsely chop the tomatoes and place them in a medium bowl. Drizzle with the oil, sprinkle with the minced parsley, and season well with salt and pepper, to taste. Toss gently to combine. Set aside.

4. Place a small spoonful of the tomato mixture into each zucchini cup and garnish with a parsley leaf. Arrange on a platter and serve or cover and refrigerate until needed.

make ahead   quick & easy

arugula and white bean crostini

MAKES ABOUT 24 CROSTINI

Crostini are the quintessential Italian appetizer—easy to make with simple fresh ingredients. The topping for this version blends creamy white beans with spunky arugula and garlic.

1 tablespoons olive oil

2 to 3 garlic cloves, minced

2 cups finely chopped arugula

2 tablespoons dry white wine or vegetable broth

1½ cups cooked or 1 (15.5-ounce) can white beans, drained and rinsed

Salt and freshly ground black pepper

1 small French baguette, cut into ½-inch-thick slices

Minced tomato, for garnish

1. In a medium saucepan heat the oil over medium heat. Add the garlic and cook until fragrant, 30 seconds. Stir in the arugula and wine and cook until wilted, about 1 minute. Mash the beans, then add them to the arugula and cook, stirring to combine. Season with salt and pepper, to taste. Keep warm over very low heat.

2. Preheat the oven to 400°F. Arrange the bread slices in a single layer on an ungreased baking sheet and toast, turning once, until lightly browned, 8 to 10 minutes. Top each of the crostini with a spoonful of the topping and garnish with tomato. Arrange on a platter and serve at once.

pesto-stuffed baby potatoes

Pesto and potatoes make a wonderful flavor combination and the little pesto-topped potatoes look adorable on a platter. Try to find the smallest potatoes available that are uniform in size in order to make this a one- or two-bite appetizer.

12 small white- or red-skinned potatoes (about 2 inches in diameter)
4 garlic cloves
⅓ cup walnut pieces

½ teaspoon salt
2 cups fresh basil leaves
¼ cup plus olive oil
Freshly ground black pepper

1. Preheat the oven to 400°F. Place the potatoes on a baking sheet and roast them until just tender, about 40 minutes.

2. While the potatoes are roasting, make the pesto: In a food processor, combine the garlic, walnuts, and salt and process until minced. Add the basil and process until finely minced. With the machine running, add the oil and process until smooth and creamy. Set aside.

3. Remove the potatoes from the oven and set aside to cool slightly. When cool enough to handle, carefully cut each of the potatoes in half. If necessary, gently cut a thin sliver off each potato to make a flat bottom. Use a melon baller or a small spoon to scoop out the inside of the potatoes and place the scooped-out potato in a bowl. Add the pesto and season with salt and pepper, to taste. Mix well.

4. Spoon the pesto-potato mixture into the potato shells and arrange on the baking sheet. Bake until hot, 10 to 15 minutes. Serve hot or warm.

make ahead   quick & easy

crowdcontrol

dessert station

coconut snowballs

These no-bake taste treats are easy to make and can be made well ahead of time for a tasty inclusion on any dessert table.

1½ cups mixed dried fruit
¾ cup sweetened dried
  cranberries
¾ cup pecans

1½ cups unsweetened shredded
  coconut
2 tablespoons fresh orange juice
Zest of 1 orange

1. In a food processor, combine the dried fruit, cranberries, and pecans and pulse until finely chopped. Add ¾ cup of the coconut, juice, and zest. Process until the mixture comes together to form a ball, about 1 minute.

2. Place the remaining ¾ cup coconut on a plate. With moist hands, shape the mixture into 1-inch balls, and roll in the shredded coconut. Arrange on a platter. If not using right away, cover tightly and store in the refrigerator or at room temperature for up to 3 days.

make ahead   **quick & easy**

crowdcontrol

cherry-pecan bars

These flavorful bar cookies taste as good as they look. Best of all, they freeze well, so you can make them well ahead of when you need them.

½ cup cherry preserves
½ cup sweetened dried cherries
½ cup coarsely chopped pecans
½ cup light brown sugar
¼ cup vegan margarine
1 teaspoon pure vanilla extract
¾ cup all-purpose flour

1 teaspoon baking powder
¼ teaspoon salt
¾ cup confectioners' sugar (for optional glaze)
2 teaspoons plain unsweetened soy milk or other nondairy milk (for optional glaze)

1. Preheat the oven to 350°F. Lightly grease an 8-inch square baking pan and set aside. In a medium bowl, combine the cherry preserves, dried cherries, and pecans. Set aside.

2. In a separate medium bowl, combine the brown sugar, margarine, and vanilla and cream together with an electric mixer on medium speed until fluffy. Stir in the flour, baking powder, and salt; mix until incorporated. Mix in preserves mixture.

3. Spread the mixture into the prepared baking pan. Bake until the top is set and golden, about 30 minutes. Cool in the pan 20 minutes, then cut into bars.

4. Transfer the cookies to a wire rack set on top of a baking pan. If using the glaze, in a small bowl, combine the confectioners' sugar and soy milk to make a thick glaze. Drizzle the glaze over the cookies. Serve at once, or cover and refrigerate for up to 3 days.

italian wedding cookies

MAKES ABOUT 4 DOZEN COOKIES

These cookies are known by many names, including Mexican wedding cookies and Russian tea cakes; my mother called them butterballs and made them without fail for every festive occasion. My mom always made them with ground walnuts, but ground almonds or pecans can be substituted. You can vary the shape from a totally round sphere, to a somewhat flattened sphere, to a crescent.

1½ cups vegan margarine
¾ cup plus ⅓ cup confectioners' sugar
¼ teaspoon salt

1½ cups finely ground walnuts
4½ teaspoons pure vanilla extract
3 cups sifted all-purpose flour

1. Preheat the oven to 325°F. In a large bowl, cream the margarine with an electric mixer on medium speed. Gradually add the ¾ cup confectioners' sugar and the salt. Beat until light and fluffy. Add the walnuts and vanilla. Blend in the flour gradually and mix well.

2. Shape into balls (or crescents), using about 1½ to 2 teaspoons for each cookie. Place on ungreased baking sheets and bake for 15 to 20 minutes. Do not brown. Cool slightly, then roll in the remaining ⅓ cup confectioners' sugar. If not using right away, store in an airtight container at room temperature.

make ahead   **quick & easy**

chocolate chunk blondies

MAKES 9 TO 12 BROWNIES

For people who waver between brownies and blondies, this recipe provides the best of both. For a variation, you can omit the chocolate and add ½ cup dried cherries and ½ cup coarsely chopped nuts (macadamias are especially good in this).

½ cup vegan margarine

1 cup firmly packed light brown sugar

½ cup plain or vanilla soy milk or other nondairy milk

1½ teaspoons pure vanilla extract

1½ cups all-purpose flour

½ teaspoon baking powder

½ teaspoon baking soda

¼ teaspoon salt

½ cup coarsely chopped vegan semisweet chocolate

1. Preheat the oven to 350°F. Lightly grease an 8-inch square baking pan and set aside. In a medium saucepan, melt the margarine over medium heat. Add the sugar and stir until blended. Remove from the heat and transfer to a medium bowl. Stir in the soy milk and vanilla and cool to room temperature.

2. In a separate medium bowl, combine the flour, baking powder, baking soda, and salt. Mix until well combined. Add the flour mixture to the sugar-soy milk mixture, stirring until well combined. Fold in the chocolate.

3. Spoon the batter into the prepared pan and spread evenly. Bake until golden brown and a toothpick inserted in the center comes out clean, 30 to 35 minutes. Remove from the oven and cool completely on a wire rack before cutting. If not using right away, store in an airtight container at room temperature or in the refrigerator for up to 3 days.

strawberries dipped in chocolate

Easy and elegant, chocolate-dipped strawberries add dramatic impact to any food display. For best results, be sure the strawberries are completely dry and at room temperature before dipping into the chocolate. Chocolate will not adhere to wet fruit. Do not allow any water to splash into the melted chocolate or it will "seize" and become grainy.

As a variation, partially dip strawberries that have been dipped in chocolate (and are already set) into melted white chocolate for a two-tone effect. Chocolate dipped strawberries are best if eaten within twenty-four hours. If not using within an hour or two, refrigerate until needed. Serve at room temperature for best flavor.

36 large fresh strawberries with leaves intact, at room temperature

1 (12-ounce) package vegan semisweet chocolate chips

2 tablespoons vegan margarine or shortening

1. Carefully wash the strawberries and pat them dry, then set aside. Line a baking sheet or cookie pan with waxed paper and set aside.

2. In a double boiler or microwave, melt the chocolate and margarine, stirring occasionally until smooth. (Do not allow any drops of water from the double boiler to get into the chocolate, which can result in "seizing.") Let the chocolate cool slightly, but do not let it set.

3. Holding the leaf end of a strawberry, dip it in the melted chocolate until it is covered about three-quarters from the top, leaving some of the berry visible. Place the dipped strawberry, stem side down, on the prepared baking sheet. Repeat with the remaining berries. Let set until the chocolate hardens, about 30 minutes. If using right away, refrigerate for 15 minutes to set the chocolate. If making ahead of time, refrigerate for up to 5 hours before serving. To serve, arrange the berries aesthetically on a serving platter.

make ahead   quick & easy

a picnic lunch

There's perhaps no better way to spend your leisure time than by enjoying the great outdoors. It can be even more fun when planned around a meal, whether you visit a local park, drive to a scenic lookout, or just stay put in your own backyard. Wherever you picnic, remember to pack the utensils, an assortment of cold drinks, and plenty of napkins.

You can also plan a picnic as a great midwinter pick-me-up. Just spread a blanket on the floor or spread a checkered tablecloth on the table. Even if there are three feet of snow outside, you can have all the fun of a summer picnic with family and friends. Best of all, no mosquito bites.

the menu

THE GREAT OUTDOORS

Southern Fried Seitan
Fingerling Potato Salad with Pan-Fried Arugula Pesto
Chilled and Dilled Green Beans
Caramel Almond-Oat Bars

Go-Withs: *watermelon, root vegetable chips; iced tea*

recipe swaps

Main Dish: Spicy-Smoky BBQ Ribz *(page 208)*

Salad: *Three-Potato Salad (page 218); or Super Slaw (page 146)*

Dessert: Man-Size Chocolate Chip Cookies *(page 149)*; or
Chocolate Lover's Brownies *(page 92)*

southern fried seitan

MAKES 4 SERVINGS

These crunchy and meaty chunks of seitan make a hearty main dish any time of year, but are especially good as a vegan alternative to that picnic staple—fried chicken.

1 cup plain unsweetened soy milk or other nondairy milk
1 tablespoon fresh lemon juice
1 teaspoon spicy brown mustard
1 tablespoon nutritional yeast
½ teaspoon salt
½ teaspoon freshly ground black pepper

¼ cup yellow cornmeal
¼ cup all-purpose flour
1½ cups panko bread crumbs
1 pound seitan, cut or torn into chunks
Neutral vegetable oil, for frying

1. In a medium bowl, combine the soy milk, lemon juice, mustard, yeast, salt, and pepper. Stir to mix well. Add the cornmeal and flour, a little at a time, stirring well to make a smooth batter. Place the panko in a shallow bowl and set aside.

2. Dip each of the seitan chunks in the batter, then dredge them in the panko.

3. In a large skillet, heat a thin layer of oil over medium-high heat. Add the seitan and cook until browned all over, about 10 minutes.

4. Transfer to a platter and serve hot or at room temperature. If not using right away, bring to room temperature, cover and refrigerate for up to 3 days, then serve at room temperature or heat in a moderate oven until hot.

make ahead   quick & easy

fingerling potato salad with pan-fried arugula pesto

MAKES 4 TO 6 SERVINGS

Garlic and arugula are two favorite ingredients that can be assertive in a good way. Sometimes, however, I'm in the mood for their great flavors, but just a little mellowed out. That's why I decided to pan-fry them for a few minutes first. It brings out the flavors, keeps the arugula a nice shade of green, and eliminates the bitterness of both—a win-win situation.

1½ pounds Yukon gold potatoes, peeled and cut into 1-inch dice
¼ cup olive oil
3 garlic cloves, crushed
2 cups fresh arugula
Salt and freshly ground black pepper

⅓ cup toasted walnut pieces
½ cup cherry or grape tomatoes, halved lengthwise
⅓ cup pitted kalamata olives, quartered lengthwise
⅓ cup finely chopped celery

1. In a large pot of boiling salted water, cook the potatoes until just tender but still firm, about 15 minutes. Drain well, reserving ½ cup of the cooking water. Transfer the potatoes to a large bowl.

2. While the potatoes are cooking, heat the oil in a skillet over medium-low heat. Add the garlic and cook for 1 minute, turning so the garlic doesn't turn brown. Add the arugula and season with salt and pepper, to taste. Cook, stirring, until just wilted, about 2 minutes. Remove from the heat and allow to cool for 5 minutes.

3. In a food processor, combine the garlic-arugula mixture, the toasted walnuts, and about ½ teaspoon salt. Process to a smooth paste. Add as much of the reserved potato water as needed to make a smooth sauce.

4. Add the pesto sauce to the potatoes. Add the tomatoes, olives, and celery and toss gently to combine. Set aside at room temperature to allow the flavors to blend, about 20 minutes. Taste and adjust the seasonings, if necessary, and serve at room temperature. If not using right away, cover and refrigerate for up to 2 days.

chilled and dilled green beans

Fresh green beans are plentiful in the summer and are especially good chilled for a picnic. Seasoning the beans with lemon and dill gives them a bright and refreshing flavor.

1 pound green beans, trimmed
1 medium shallot, minced
1 tablespoon fresh lemon juice
3 tablespoons fresh coarsely
 chopped dill weed

¼ teaspoon sugar
¼ teaspoon salt
⅛ teaspoon freshly ground black
 pepper
2 tablespoons olive oil

1. Steam the green beans until crisp-tender, 5 to 7 minutes. Rinse under cold water and place in a shallow bowl. Set aside.

2. In a small bowl, combine the shallot, lemon juice, dill weed, sugar, salt, and pepper. Add the oil, stirring until blended. Pour the dressing over the green beans and toss gently to coat. Cover and refrigerate for at least 4 hours before serving.

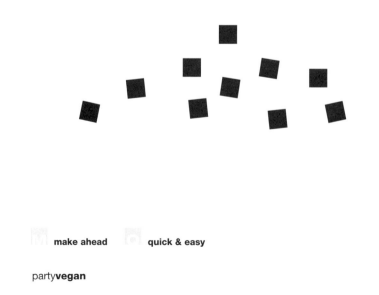

make ahead　　**quick & easy**

caramel almond-oat bars

Easy to make and oh so satisfying, these tasty bars are hard to resist. Keep them stashed in a container in the bottom of your picnic basket to avoid raiding them on the way to your destination.

BARS

½ cup vegan margarine, melted

½ cup almond butter

¼ cup pure maple syrup

½ cup light brown sugar

½ teaspoon salt

1 teaspoon pure vanilla extract

1 cup old-fashioned oats, ground to a powder

¾ cup all-purpose flour

1 teaspoon baking powder

½ cup slivered raw almonds

CARAMEL

¼ cup plain or vanilla soy milk or other nondairy milk

1 tablespoon arrowroot powder

¼ cup vegan margarine

½ cup light brown sugar

3 tablespoons pure maple syrup

1. Preheat the oven to 375°F. Lightly grease an 8-inch square baking pan and set aside.

2. Make the bars: In a medium saucepan, combine the margarine, almond butter, maple syrup, sugar, and salt. Stir until the margarine is melted and the sugar is dissolved. Remove from the heat and stir in the vanilla. Transfer to a medium bowl and set aside.

3. In a separate medium bowl, combine the oats, flour, and baking powder and mix until well blended. Stir the dry mixture into the wet mixture. Add half the almonds and mix until well combined. Press the dough into the prepared pan. Sprinkle the remaining almonds over the top and press them into the dough. Bake until browned, 25 to 30 minutes.

4. Make the caramel: In a small bowl, combine the soy milk with the arrowroot and set aside. In a medium saucepan, combine the margarine and sugar and heat over medium heat until the margarine is melted and the sugar is dissolved. Stir in the maple syrup and bring to a boil over high heat.

Remove from the heat and stir in the arrowroot mixture to thicken. Set aside to cool.

5. When the bars are done baking, let them cool for 15 minutes, then drizzle the top with the caramel and refrigerate to set up, about 1 hour. When completely cool, cut into bars. If not using right away, transfer to an airtight container and refrigerate for up to 3 days.

effortless potluck

Perhaps the easiest way to entertain is to host a potluck. It's a fun way to have a party with a minimum amount of work and expense. People enjoy sampling a little taste of what everyone brings, and talking about the different dishes can make for good conversation. When everyone in your group brings something to the table, the results can be wonderful, both in taste and in the distribution of labor—no one has to work too hard and everyone gets to taste a variety of dishes.

Unlike the other chapters in this book, which include recipes for a single menu, this chapter features individual dishes that can be made to bring to a potluck meal—whether you're the host or an invited guest. Any of these tried-and-true favorites would be a welcome addition to a potluck feast and the recipes can also be tapped for easy family meals anytime.

the menu

POTLUCK FAVORITES

Spiced Chickpea and Couscous Pilaf
Very Veggie Lasagna
Two-Potato Shepherd's Pie
Antipasto Rice
Creamy Noodle and Vegetable Bake

recipe swaps

Consider any of these recipes when looking for a main dish to swap out in the other menus in this book. For example, the lasagna can be prepared as the main dish for the Company's Coming menu on page 37 and the Antipasto Rice can be enjoyed as part of the picnic menu on page 73, to replace one or more of the other recipes.

spiced chickpea and couscous pilaf

MAKES 6 SERVINGS

Redolent of fragrant spices and filled with great textures and flavors, this colorful pilaf is a secret weapon you can serve for almost any gathering. Made with pantry ingredients and assembled in minutes, it's wonderful in its own right, but it also comes in handy for whipping up at the last minute if extra guests arrive or as a last-minute replacement if another dish is a no-show. Keep this in mind for a quick and easy weeknight meal anytime.

1 tablespoon olive oil
1 red bell pepper, minced
3 green onions, minced
1 large carrot, shredded
½ teaspoon ground coriander
½ teaspoon ground cumin
⅛ teaspoon ground allspice
3 cups vegetable broth
1 tablespoon nutritional yeast
(optional)

1½ cups or 1 (15.5-ounce) can
chickpeas, drained and rinsed
1½ cups couscous
1 cup frozen baby peas, thawed
Salt and freshly ground black
pepper
¼ cup golden raisins
¼ cup shelled pistachios
2 tablespoons minced fresh
parsley

1. In a large skillet, heat the oil over medium heat. Add the bell pepper, green onions, and carrot. Cook, stirring, until softened, about 3 minutes. Add the coriander, cumin, allspice, broth, and yeast, if using, and bring to a boil. Stir in the chickpeas, couscous, and peas. Season with salt and black pepper, to taste. Cover and remove from the heat. Set aside for 10 minutes.

2. Transfer pilaf to a serving bowl. Gently stir in the raisins, pistachios, and parsley. Serve immediately. If not using right away, bring to room temperature, cover, and refrigerate for up to 2 days, then reheat when needed.

make ahead   **quick & easy**

very veggie lasagna

Everyone loves lasagna, which makes it a great choice for a pot-luck. Layered with noodles, sauce, and a rich vegetable and tofu filling, this lasagna also makes a great one-dish meal.

1 tablespoon olive oil
1 medium yellow onion, finely chopped
3 garlic cloves, minced
½ cup finely chopped red bell pepper
2 cups coarsely chopped white mushrooms
1 medium zucchini, coarsely chopped
1 (10-ounce) package frozen chopped spinach, thawed

¾ teaspoon salt
1 pound soft tofu, drained and crumbled
3 tablespoons nutritional yeast
¼ cup minced fresh parsley
1 teaspoon dried basil
¼ teaspoon dried marjoram
¼ teaspoon freshly ground black pepper
8 ounces lasagna noodles
3½ cups marinara sauce
Vegan Parmesan or mozzarella

1. In a large skillet, heat the oil over medium heat. Add the onion, cover, and cook until softened, 5 minutes. Uncover, stir in the garlic, bell pepper, mushrooms, and zucchini and cook, stirring occasionally, until the vegetables are softened, about 5 minutes. Add the spinach and about ¼ teaspoon of the salt and cook, stirring, until the vegetables are well combined. Remove from the heat and set aside.

2. In a large bowl, combine the tofu with the yeast, parsley, basil, marjoram, black pepper, and the remaining ½ teaspoon of salt. Mix well. Add the reserved vegetable mixture and stir well to combine. Taste and adjust the seasonings, if necessary. Set aside.

3. In a pot of boiling salted water, cook the noodles over medium-high heat, stirring occasionally, until al dente, about 7 minutes. Drain and set aside. Preheat the oven to 350°F.

make ahead   **quick & easy**

4. To assemble, spread a layer of tomato sauce in the bottom of a 9 x 13-inch baking pan. Top the sauce with a layer of noodles. Top the noodles with half of the tofu-vegetable mixture, spreading evenly. Repeat with another layer of noodles and top with more sauce. Spread the remaining tofu-vegetable mixture on top, followed by a layer of noodles and sauce. Sprinkle the vegan cheese on top.

5. Cover with foil and bake for 50 minutes. Uncover and bake another 10 minutes. Remove from the oven and serve hot. If not serving right away, cover the unbaked lasagne tightly with foil and refrigerate for up to 2 days, then bring to room temperature before baking as directed.

tried and true

I make it a policy not to debut an untried new dish for company, and I encourage you to do likewise. If you're not making familiar favorites, then try to give any new recipe a practice run before the actual company meal. This also allows you the opportunity to adjust any of the seasonings so it suits your needs, as well as to get a visual fix on the yield and appearance of the finished dish. Knowing in advance what to expect from a particular recipe will help eliminate the stress factor when you make it the second time around, because by then, you're an expert.

two-potato shepherd's pie

MAKES 8 SERVINGS

A hearty shepherd's pie is a welcome addition to a potluck table.

3 tablespoon olive oil

1 large yellow onion, chopped

2 medium carrots, chopped

2 garlic cloves, minced

1½ cups chopped white
mushrooms

2 cups chopped seitan

1 cup fresh or thawed frozen
corn kernels

1 cup frozen peas

1 cup cooked green beans, cut
into 1-inch pieces (optional)

Salt and black pepper

3 tablespoons all-purpose flour

2½ cups vegetable broth

2 tablespoons soy sauce

1 teaspoon minced fresh thyme
or ½ teaspoon dried

1 teaspoon minced fresh
marjoram or ½ teaspoon dried

2 large Yukon gold or russet
potatoes, peeled and cut into
½-inch dice

2 sweet potatoes, peeled and
cut into ½-inch dice

2 tablespoons vegan margarine

1. Preheat the oven to 350°F. Lightly oil a 9 x 13-baking pan and set aside. In a large saucepan, heat 1 tablespoon of the oil over medium heat. Add the onion and carrots. Cover and cook until softened, about 10 minutes. Uncover and add the garlic and mushrooms. Cook, stirring occasionally, until softened, about 4 minutes. Stir in the seitan, corn, peas, and green beans, if using. Season with salt and pepper, to taste. Transfer the mixture the prepared pan, spread evenly, set aside.

2. In a medium saucepan, heat the remaining oil over medium heat. Add the flour and cook, stirring, for 30 seconds. Stir in the broth, soy sauce, thyme, marjoram, and salt and pepper, to taste. Cook, stirring, until the sauce thickens, about 3 minutes. Pour the sauce over the filling mixture, mix well, and set aside.

3. Steam the white potatoes and sweet potatoes separately. When soft, transfer to separate bowls. Add 1 tablespoon margarine to each bowl of potatoes and season with salt and pepper, to taste. Mash the white potatoes and spread evenly on one-half of the filling. Mash the sweet potatoes and spread them evenly on the other half of the filling. Bake until hot and bubbly, 30 to 40 minutes. Serve hot. If not using right away, cover and refrigerate for up to 2 days. Bring to room temperature before baking.

antipasto rice

Colorful and vibrant, this flavorful dish is best served at room temperature, making it ideal for a potluck meal. It's also versatile: you can eliminate one of the vegetables or add others.

4 tablespoons olive oil

1 celery rib, cut into ¼-inch slices

1 small zucchini, coarsely chopped

3 garlic cloves, minced

3 green onions, minced

6 ounces white mushrooms, lightly rinsed, patted dry, and cut into ¼-inch slices

½ teaspoon minced fresh oregano

1½ cups cooked or 1 (15.5-ounce) can chickpeas, drained and rinsed

1 cup canned unmarinated or cooked frozen artichokes hearts, coarsely chopped

1 roasted red bell pepper, coarsely chopped

3 cups cold cooked long-grain brown rice

1 cup ripe grape tomatoes, halved

½ cup kalamata olives, pitted and halved

2 tablespoons minced oil-packed sun-dried tomatoes

2 tablespoons capers, drained and rinsed

2 tablespoons coarsely chopped fresh parsley

2 tablespoons coarsely chopped fresh basil

2 tablespoons white balsamic vinegar

½ teaspoon sugar

½ teaspoon salt

⅛ teaspoon freshly ground black pepper

1. In a large skillet, heat 1 tablespoon of the oil over medium heat. Add the celery and zucchini. Cook until softened, about 3 minutes. Add the garlic, green onions, and mushrooms. Cook, stirring to soften, about 2 minutes. Stir in the oregano, chickpeas, artichokes, and bell pepper. Cook for 1 minute and set aside.

2. In a large serving bowl, combine the rice, grape tomatoes, olives, sun-dried tomatoes, capers, parsley, and the vegetable mixture. Drizzle with the remaining 3 tablespoons oil. Add the vinegar, sugar, salt, and black pepper and toss to combine. Set aside for 20 minutes to allow flavors to combine. If not serving right away, cover and refrigerate until needed. Bring to room temperature before serving.

make ahead   **quick & easy**

creamy noodle and vegetable bake

This mellow comfort-food casserole is rich and flavorful and ideal for potlucks or anytime you want an easy one-dish meal that can be assembled ahead of time and then heated when ready to serve. Kids love this dish, too, although you'll want to leave out the sherry if making it for children.

8 ounces fettuccine, broken into thirds

2 tablespoons olive oil

1 large yellow onion, coarsely chopped

2 medium carrots, coarsely chopped

1 celery rib, coarsely chopped

8 ounces white mushrooms, lightly rinsed, patted dry, and cut into ¼-inch slices

4 ounces green beans, trimmed, cut into 1-inch pieces, and steamed

1 cup cooked cannellini beans

½ cup frozen peas, thawed

¼ cup vegan margarine

¼ cup all-purpose flour

2½ cups vegetable broth

3 tablespoons minced fresh parsley

1 teaspoon dried thyme

1 teaspoon smoked paprika

½ teaspoon dried marjoram

1 cup plain unsweetened soy milk or other nondairy milk

⅓ cup dry sherry

Salt and freshly ground black pepper

½ cup panko bread crumbs

1. Preheat the oven to 350°F. Lightly oil a 9 x 13-inch baking pan and set aside. Cook the fettuccine in a pot of boiling salted water until al dente, about 10 minutes. Drain and return to the pot. Set aside.

2. In a large skillet, heat 1 tablespoon of the oil over medium heat. Add the onion, carrots, and celery. Cover and cook until softened, about 5 minutes. Uncover and stir in the mushrooms and cook until softened, about 4 minutes. Remove from the heat and stir in the green beans, cannellini beans, and peas. Add the vegetable mixture to the noodles and set aside.

3. In a medium saucepan, melt the margarine over medium heat and quickly whisk in the flour. Slowly whisk in the broth. Add the parsley, thyme,

½ teaspoon of the paprika, marjoram, soy milk, and sherry. Season with salt and pepper, to taste, and cook, stirring, until thickened, 2 to 3 minutes.

4. Add the sauce to the noodle-vegetable mixture and stir gently to combine. Transfer the mixture to the prepared baking pan, spreading evenly. Cover and bake for 30 minutes.

5. In a small bowl, combine the panko with the remaining 1 tablespoon oil, the remaining ½ teaspoon paprika, and salt and pepper, to taste. Remove the pan from the oven, uncover, and sprinkle with the panko mixture. Return to the oven and bake, uncovered, until the crumbs are nicely browned, about 10 minutes. Serve hot. If not using right away, the casserole can be assembled, tightly covered, and refrigerated for up to 2 days. Bring to room temperature before baking or bake about 15 minutes longer to make sure it is hot all the way through.

make ahead   quick & easy

A potluck is an ideal way to entertain when you are short on time, money, or both, since the expense and work involved are divided among you and your guests. Still, there are a number of things to remember when hosting a potluck that will help it come off without a hitch. Here are ten tips to use next time you host a potluck:

1. As the host, you will be providing a welcoming location for the party by opening your home to guests. In addition, you should also plan on providing the plates, silverware, napkins, and glasses, as well as bar mixers (if needed) and a main dish.

2. To begin, make a list (by category) of the foods you would like your guests to bring, such as appetizer, salad, main dish, side dish, bread, dessert, and beverage. Assign a type of dish to each guest, soliciting suggestions for specifics. Make sure the menu includes a variety of hot, cold, and room temperature foods—if it's all hot food, everyone will be vying for oven space. Keep track of the foods in terms of both type and temperature to avoid repetition and create a good balance.

3. If guests don't know what to bring, be ready with specific suggestions to fill in any menu gaps. For example, if a particular guest makes a special dish, ask them to bring it. Without this kind of organization, there is a potential that everyone will bring a jar of pickles or a bag of pretzels.

4. If any of your guests are cooking-challenged, suggest that they bring the bread or rolls, beverages, or snack foods.

5. Ask guests to bring a serving utensil appropriate to the dish they are bringing. (If they don't, you're bound to run out of large serving spoons within seconds and you may end up dishing everything out with plastic teaspoons. (This actually happened at a party I attended.)

6. Let your guests know how many people are attending and that you need them to bring enough of their particular item to serve that number of people.

7. Be sure guests know what time to arrive so that all the food can be set out at the same time. All the dishes should be ready to serve and kept at the proper temperature until placed on the table. Until serving time, keep cold foods refrigerated and hot foods warming in the oven. Be sure you have enough hot plates for your table.

8. Ask guests to tape their names to their serving dishes and utensils for easy identification at the end of the party.

9. Check with guests to accommodate any food allergies, and let others know about your own allergies if you have them. Consider asking guests to bring copies of their recipes or at least lists of ingredients. Even people without allergies enjoy knowing what ingredients are in a dish.

10. If possible, wash your guests' containers before they leave so they can take them home. Otherwise, make sure the containers are clearly marked, or make a list to keep track. Have some disposable food storage containers on hand so guests can take home leftovers.

just
desserts

A dessert buffet is a fun way to entertain. After all, everyone loves dessert and this kind of entertaining takes the pressure off providing dinner for your guests. Because you can basically put everything out all at once and let people dig in, a dessert buffet allows you to relax and enjoy the party from start to finish.

On a practical note, be sure to let your guests know in advance that this is a dessert party, so they don't arrive hungry and expecting to be served a complete meal. Since these desserts are made without eggs or dairy products, even folks watching their cholesterol will be able to dig in with abandon. Still, it's a good idea to include some fresh fruit on the menu for those counting calories.

Depending on the crowd and time of day or evening, plan to serve the desserts with coffee or champagne—or both! During the summer months, you may want to serve a chilled punch or iced tea. In the winter, warm cider is a good choice.

the menu

DESSERT, EVERYONE?

Chocolate Lover's Brownies
Pine Nut–Anise Cookies
Ginger-Spice Cupcakes
Pistachio-Dusted Chocolate-Raspberry Truffles
Fresh Berry Tartlets
Fresh Fruit Picks with Two Dips

Go-Withs: *for special occasions, order a personalized bakery cake as a centerpiece; coffee and champagne or punch (alcoholic or non)*

recipe swaps

This menu consists of pickup desserts—no fork or spoon necessary. Other no-fork dessert recipes that can work with this menu can include: Tres Leches Cupcakes (page 195); Cherry-Pecan Bars (page 68); Italian Wedding Cookies (page 69); Chocolate Chunk Blondies (page 70); Caramel Almond-Oat Bars (page 77); Coconut Snowballs (page 67); or Strawberries Dipped in Chocolate (page 71).

If your party marks a special occasion, such as a birthday or graduation, you may want to include a deco-rated cake as a centerpiece, in which case, you'll need the forks.

chocolate lover's brownies

If you love chocolate, you'll adore these brownies made with a double dose of chocolate in the form of cocoa and chocolate chips.

½ cup applesauce

¼ cup pure maple syrup

¼ cup plain or vanilla soy milk or other nondairy milk

¼ cup neutral vegetable oil

1 teaspoon pure vanilla extract

1 cup all-purpose flour

¾ cup sugar

½ cup unsweetened cocoa powder

1 teaspoon baking powder

¼ teaspoon salt

½ cup vegan semisweet chocolate chips

½ cup coarsely chopped walnuts (optional)

1. Preheat the oven to 350°F. Lightly grease an 8-inch square baking pan.

2. In a large bowl, combine the applesauce, maple syrup, soy milk, oil, and vanilla and whisk to combine.

3. In a separate large bowl, whisk together the flour, sugar, cocoa, baking powder, and salt.

4. Fold the dry ingredients into the wet mixture with a rubber spatula. Don't overmix. Fold in the chocolate chips and walnuts, if using.

5. Scrape the batter into the pan and spread it evenly. Bake for 35 minutes. Cool for 30 minutes in the pan on a wire rack before cutting. If not serving right away, cover tightly and store at room temperature. These brownies taste best if eaten within a day or two.

pine nut–anise cookies

Not too sweet, these fragrant and flavorful cookies make a so-phisticated addition to any dessert table. Both the cookie dough and the baked cookies freeze well.

½ cup vegan margarine

¼ cup confectioners' sugar

½ teaspoon pure vanilla extract

¾ teaspoon anise extract

1 cup all-purpose flour

⅛ teaspoon salt

¼ cup coarsely ground pine nuts

2 tablespoons whole pine nuts

1. In a large bowl, combine the margarine and sugar and cream together with an electric mixer on medium speed until light and fluffy. Beat in the vanilla and anise extract. Stir in the flour, salt, and ground pine nuts. Wrap dough in plastic and refrigerate until chilled, about 1 hour.

2. Preheat the oven to 325°F. Lightly grease a large baking sheet and set aside.

3. Pinch off the dough in 1-inch pieces and roll them into balls. (The dough may be crumbly.) Place the dough balls on the prepared baking sheet. Flatten slightly. Press about 3 whole pine nuts into the top of each cookie. Bake until lightly golden, about 20 minutes. Remove to wire racks to cool. Store, covered, at room temperature for up to 2 days or wrap tightly and freeze for up to 2 weeks. If frozen, thaw completely before serving.

make ahead　　**quick & easy**

ginger-spice cupcakes

Everyone loves cupcakes and you'll especially love how easy they are to serve at a party—no messy slicing and serving is needed since everyone gets their own personal cake.

CUPCAKES

¾ cup plain or vanilla soy milk or other nondairy milk

1½ teaspoons apple cider vinegar

1¼ cups all-purpose flour

1 teaspoon baking powder

¼ teaspoon baking soda

¼ teaspoon salt

1 teaspoon ground ginger

¼ teaspoon ground cinnamon

¼ teaspoon ground allspice

⅛ teaspoon ground nutmeg or cloves

½ cup granulated sugar

¼ cup light brown sugar

¼ cup neutral vegetable oil

1½ teaspoons pure vanilla extract

FROSTING

1 cup vegan margarine

4 cups confectioners' sugar

2 tablespoons plain or vanilla soy milk or other nondairy milk

¾ teaspoon ground ginger

¼ teaspoon ground cinnamon

¼ teaspoon ground allspice, nutmeg, or cloves

1½ teaspoons pure vanilla extract

Slivers of candied ginger, for garnish

1. Make the cupcakes: Preheat the oven to 350°F. Lightly grease a 12-cup muffin tin or line with paper liners. Set aside.

2. In a small bowl, combine the soy milk and vinegar and set aside. In a medium bowl, combine the flour, baking powder, baking soda, salt, ginger, cinnamon, allspice, and nutmeg. Mix to combine.

3. In a large bowl, combine both the sugars, oil, and vanilla. Stir in the soy milk mixture. Add the dry ingredients to the wet ingredients and stir until smooth.

4. Pour the batter evenly into the prepared tin about two-thirds full and bake until a toothpick inserted in the center of a cupcake comes out clean, about 20 minutes. Cool completely on a wire rack before frosting.

5. Make the frosting: In a large bowl, cream the margarine with an electric mixer on high speed until light and fluffy. Add the confectioners' sugar, soy milk, spices, and vanilla and mix until thoroughly combined. Continue mixing for about 2 minutes until the frosting is smooth and stiff.

6. When the cupcakes are completely cool, frost them with the frosting. Top each cupcake with a sliver of candied ginger.

make ahead　　**quick & easy**

pistachio-dusted chocolate-raspberry truffles

MAKES ABOUT 3 DOZEN

These decadent bites can be made up to two weeks in advance and frozen until needed. Allow to thaw completely before serving.

8 ounces vegan semisweet chocolate

5 tablespoons vegan margarine

⅓ cup seedless raspberry preserves

⅓ cup finely chopped shelled unsalted pistachios

2 tablespoons plain or vanilla soy milk or other nondairy milk

½ cup finely ground unsalted pistachios, for coating

1. Melt the chocolate and margarine in a double boiler or microwave until smooth. Remove from the heat. Stir in the preserves, chopped pistachios, and soy milk. Transfer to a medium bowl. Cover and refrigerate until firm, about 30 minutes.

2. Use a teaspoon to scoop about ¾ teaspoon of the mixture and use your hands to shape it into a ¾-inch ball. Repeat with the remaining mixture and roll the balls in the ground pistachios. Arrange them on a platter or place in small foil or paper candy cups and serve.

make ahead   **quick & easy**

fresh berry tartlets

These pretty tartlets are easy to make and quite versatile. You can use one kind of berry or mix and match two or three varieties. You can save time by using a graham cracker or other cookie crumb crust. For a lovely finish, you can dust the tartlets with confectioners' sugar, or glaze them with melted apple jelly, or use neither and simply garnish each with a mint leaf. The tartlets can be assembled up to 3 hours in advance and stored at room temperature. (If garnishing with confectioners' sugar, dust the tartlets just prior to serving.)

CRUST

1¼ cups all-purpose flour

¼ teaspoon salt

1 teaspoon granulated sugar

½ cup vegan margarine, cut into small pieces

3 tablespoons ice water

FILLING

6 ounces vegan cream cheese

½ cup granulated sugar

1 teaspoon pure vanilla extract

1½ cups fresh berries (raspberries, blueberries, blackberries, or small or halved strawberries)

½ cup apple jelly (optional)

Confectioners' sugar (optional)

Fresh mint leaves (optional)

1. Make the crust: In a food processor, combine the flour, salt, and granulated sugar and pulse to combine. Add the margarine and process until crumbly. With the machine running, add the water and process to form a dough. Do not overmix. Flatten the dough into a disk.

2. Roll out the dough on a lightly floured work surface to about ⅛ inch thick. Use a small round pastry cutter or drinking glass (about 1½ to 2 inches in diameter) and cut as many rounds as you can from the dough (you should get about 20). Fit the dough rounds into small tartlet pans or mini muffin tins. Trim the edges and prick holes in the bottom of each tartlet with a fork.

Refrigerate for 20 minutes. Preheat the oven to 400°F. Line each tartlet with a small piece of parchment paper or aluminum foil and fill with dried beans. Bake for 10 minutes, then remove the paper and beans and bake until crisp and golden, about 10 minutes longer. Set aside to cool completely.

3. Make the filling: In a food processor, combine the cream cheese, granulated sugar, and vanilla, and process until smooth. Spoon the mixture into the baked tartlets. Arrange the berries on top.

4. If a glaze is desired, melt the apple jelly in a small saucepan and use a pastry brush to lightly paint the tops of the fruit. If using confectioners' sugar, dust the tartlets just prior to serving. If a mint garnish is desired, nestle a small mint leaf next to the fruit on top of each tartlet just prior to serving.

make ahead   **quick & easy**

fresh fruit picks with two dips

MAKES ABOUT 2 DOZEN SKEWERS

These colorful fruit picks are a refreshing addition to the dessert buffet and a good idea to include on your menu for people who are avoiding sweets. For those who enjoy a bit of decadence with their fruit, there are two luscious sauces to choose from.

CHOCOLATE-FRAMBOISE SAUCE

½ cup agave nectar

½ cup unsweetened cocoa powder

3 tablespoons framboise liqueur (see note on page 100)

LEMON-CASHEW SAUCE

1 cup unsalted raw cashews

⅓ cup pure maple syrup or agave nectar

¼ cup fresh lemon juice

1 teaspoon pure vanilla extract

¼ cup firm silken tofu, drained and crumbled

¼ cup plain or vanilla soy milk or other nondairy milk

1 teaspoon grated lemon zest

FRUIT

12 ripe medium strawberries, hulled

2 cups fresh or canned (1-inch) pineapple chunks

12 ripe small Italian plums, halved and pitted

2 large navel oranges, peeled and cut into 1-inch pieces

1. Make the chocolate-framboise sauce: In a small saucepan, combine the agave nectar and cocoa, stirring until well combined. Bring to a simmer over low heat, cooking for about 1 minute, stirring constantly so the cocoa does not burn. Remove from the heat and stir in the framboise, stirring until well blended. Transfer to a bowl to serve.

2. Make the lemon-cashew sauce: In a blender, grind the cashews to a fine powder. Add the maple syrup, lemon juice, and vanilla and process until smooth. Add the tofu, soy milk, and zest and process until smooth and creamy. Taste and adjust the seasonings, adding more maple syrup or juice if needed. Transfer to a bowl to serve.

3. Make the fruit: Skewer the fruit alternately onto wooden skewers or toothpicks and arrange them decoratively on a platter. Serve with the sauces.

Note: If you don't want to use framboise, you can use other liqueur such as Frangelico or amaretto. For a nonalcoholic version, use soy milk, coconut milk, or fruit juice in place of the liqueur.

a child's birthday party

Aside from the cleanup, one of the biggest challenges of throwing a child's birthday party is keeping the sugar level down to a dull roar. This menu keeps the kids busy and also let's them "play" with their food. Best of all, sweets are kept to a minimum.

You will notice that two of the menu items involve "hands-on" participation. Whether you think this is a good idea or not will depend on the ages and temperaments of the children involved and just how messy you want your kitchen to be afterward. You probably only want to do this if you have another adult helping with supervision and limit the number of children to those who can easily fit around your table or kitchen counter.

On the plus side, letting kids help to make their own personal pizza and ice cream sundae provides entertainment for the children and keeps them busy doing something constructive. Since kids are usually more likely to eat something they've had a hand in, they'll enjoy chowing down on their masterpieces.

the menu

CHILD'S PLAY

It's My Party Mix
Personal Pizzas
Mutant Ants on a Log
Build-Your-Own Ice Cream Sundaes

Go-Withs: chips, pretzels, a birthday cake; fruit punch

recipe swaps

In place of pizzas: serve Independence Burgers
(page 217) and Three-Potato Salad (page 218).
Dessert: Coconut Snowballs (page 67) or Chocolate
Chunk Blondies (page 70).

it's my party mix

A bowl of crunchy party mix is a fun addition to any party. You can vary the ingredients as you please, but I like this version because it's a nice balance of salty and sweet, crunchy and chewy.

4 cups popped popcorn

2 cups rice or corn cereal squares

¼ cup vegan margarine

2 tablespoons light brown sugar

¼ teaspoon salt

1 cup small pretzels

1 cup unsalted roasted peanuts

¾ cup golden raisins

¾ cup vegan semisweet chocolate chips

1. Preheat the oven to 250°F. In a 9 x 13-inch baking pan, combine the popcorn and cereal.

2. In a small saucepan, combine the margarine, sugar, and salt. Cook over medium heat, stirring to melt the margarine and dissolve the sugar, 1 to 2 minutes. Drizzle over the popcorn mixture, stirring to mix well. Bake for 40 minutes, stirring occasionally. Cool completely, stirring occasionally, about 30 minutes.

3. Transfer the cooled mixture to a large bowl. Add the pretzels, peanuts, raisins, and chocolate chips and toss gently to combine. If not using right away, cover tightly and store at room temperature.

make ahead   **quick & easy**

personal pizzas

Kids of all ages will love having their own personal pizza. Depending on the ages and number of children, you can involve them in "helping" get the pizzas ready for baking by letting them choose their own toppings and even arrange them on the pizza dough.

The secret to getting these pizzas in and out of the oven quickly is to partially bake the crusts ahead of time. Depending on your choice of toppings, if using raw vegetables such as mushrooms or bell peppers, you might want to sauté them ahead of time to soften since they won't be in the oven on the pizza for more than a few minutes.

DOUGH

3 cups all-purpose flour

2½ teaspoons active dry yeast

1 teaspoon salt

1 cup plus 2 tablespoons luke-warm water

TOPPINGS

Marinara sauce

Dried oregano

Shredded vegan mozzarella

Sliced white mushrooms

Chopped yellow bell pepper

Sliced cherry tomatoes

Sliced pitted olives

1. Make the dough: In a large bowl, combine the flour, yeast, and salt. Stir in the water until combined, then use your hands to knead it into dough.

2. Transfer the dough to a lightly floured work surface and knead until it is smooth and elastic, about 10 minutes. Shape the dough into a smooth ball and place in an oiled bowl. Cover with plastic wrap and let rise at room temperature in a warm spot until nearly double in size, about 1 hour.

3. After the dough has risen, transfer it to a floured work surface, punch it down, and divide it into 8 to 10 small balls (depending on your preference for a thick or thin crust). Gently stretch and shape each dough ball to make a ¼- to ⅛-inch-thick round crust about 5 to 6 inches in diameter.

4. Transfer the crusts to floured baking sheets and let rise in draft-free place for 20 minutes. Place the oven rack in the bottom-most position of the oven. Preheat the oven to 425°F. Prebake the crusts (in batches) for about 7 minutes. Remove from the oven and set aside.

5. Spread a thin layer of marinara sauce on top of each pizza round. Sprinkle with oregano. Top each pizza with the desired toppings and bake until the crust is browned, 5 to 6 minutes. Serve immediately. The crusts may be prebaked several hours in advance and then cooled and covered until needed. Refrigerate if making more than a few hours ahead. The toppings may be sautéed up to a day in advance, then covered and refrigerated. Bring to room temperature before baking.

last-minute rescues

If you think this hands-on approach would be more stressful (or messy) than you would like, then you can simply make the pizzas yourself and serve them. Instead of personal pizzas, you can make large pizzas and cut them into small pieces.

The ice cream sundae idea is also a lot of fun when just a few children are involved and they're old enough to participate. Otherwise, just scoop the ice cream yourself to serve with the birthday cake, or omit it entirely.

105

make ahead   quick & easy

mutant ants on a log

MAKES 30 TO 40 LOGS

Kids of all ages love "ants on a log" and using different-colored dried fruit makes the ants look like "mutants" and adds to the fun. Best of all, this is one snack that's made with healthful ingredients—so it's a win-win for everyone.

10 to 12 celery ribs
1 cup creamy peanut butter
2 teaspoons pure maple syrup
¼ cup sweetened dried
  cranberries

¼ cup sweetened dried
  blueberries

1. Trim the ends from the celery and, using a vegetable peeler or sharp paring knife, remove a thin strip from along the back of each celery rib so they lie flat without wobbling. Set aside.

2. In a medium bowl, combine the peanut butter and maple syrup, stirring to blend well.

3. Stuff the peanut butter mixture into each celery rib, spreading evenly with a knife so the peanut butter mixture is flush with the top of the celery. Gently press the cranberries and blueberries into the peanut butter. Cut the celery into 2-inch-long pieces and arrange on a platter and serve. If not using right away, cover and refrigerate for up to 2 days in advance.

build-your-own ice cream sundaes

How "hands-on" you want this to be will depend on the age and number of children involved. For younger children, you might want to limit the ice cream to one flavor and give them each one small scoop in a bowl. You can then help them customize their own sundae by offering just a few toppings that you can put on for them. Alternatively, make the sundaes according to your own preference and serve them—or just serve a scoop of ice cream alongside the birthday cake.

2 or 3 pints vegan ice cream (variety of flavors)

■ TOPPINGS

Fruit: sliced strawberries, sliced bananas, blueberries, etc.

Nuts: crushed peanuts, chopped walnuts, sliced almonds, etc.

Sauces: chocolate sauce, vegan whipped cream, strawberry sauce, etc.

1. Soften the ice cream at room temperature until soft enough to scoop easily. Scoop the ice cream and arrange the scoops on a baking sheet lined with plastic wrap. Place the ice cream in the freezer to let the scoops re-harden. If not serving right away, cover the ice cream tightly with plastic wrap.

2. When ready to serve, transfer each flavor of ice cream scoops to a shallow bowl and place it inside a larger bowl lined with ice cubes to help keep the ice cream from melting. Place the various toppings in small bowls. Arrange the ice cream and toppings on the table along with dessert bowls and spoons. Allow guests to "build their own" ice cream sundaes.

make ahead   **quick & easy**

a teen party

When children get older, they are more inclined to want to plan their own parties. This menu offers some tasty dishes that teens and parents alike can agree on. While the role most teens want their parents to play is a disappearing act, with a menu like this, they're sure to welcome your presence—as long as you keep the food coming.

Although I've framed this menu as a teen party, the fact is that it can work for a casual grown-up get-together, too. And like many of the menus in this book, you don't need to make all the recipes to have a great party. For example, you can skip the taco bar entirely and just serve the potato skins, wingz, and bean dip. Add some chips, salsa, and your favorite beverages and let's party!

the menu

LET'S PARTY

Baked Potato Skins
Five-Story Bean Dip
Seitan Buffalo Wingz
Ultimate Taco Bar
Everyone's Favorite Ice Cream Cake

Go-Withs: *tortilla chips, salsa; nonalcoholic punch*

recipe swaps

For the wingz: *Spinach-Potato Quesadillas (page 189)*

Dip: *Vegetable Dippers with Ranch Dressing (page 210)*

Instead of the taco bar: *Independence Burgers (page 217)*

Dessert: *Chocolate Lover's Brownies (page 92)*

baked potato skins

These potato skins are so good, they're reason enough to throw a party and guaranteed to be a big hit. Keep them in mind anytime you want something easy and delicious to serve at a casual get-together. They can be assembled ahead of time, then covered and refrigerated until it's time to pop them in the oven to heat and serve.

12 small new potatoes
Olive oil
½ cup vegan sour cream
2 tablespoons nutritional yeast
¼ cup finely minced cooked
  vegan bacon

2 tablespoons finely minced
  green onions
½ teaspoon salt
¼ teaspoon freshly ground black
  pepper
¼ teaspoon smoked paprika,
  plus more for garnish

1. Preheat the oven to 400°F. Pierce the potatoes with a fork, arrange on a baking sheet in a single layer, and brush with the oil. Roast until tender, 40 to 45 minutes. Set aside to cool.

2. When cool enough to handle, cut the potatoes in half. Use a teaspoon to scoop out and reserve most of the potato, leaving about a ¼-inch edge intact. Place the potato skins on the baking sheet and set aside.

3. In a bowl, mash the reserved potato. Add the sour cream, yeast, bacon, green onions, salt, pepper, and paprika. Spoon a small amount of the mixture into each potato skin and sprinkle each with paprika. Bake until golden on top, about 15 minutes.

make ahead   **quick & easy**

five-story bean dip

Layers of flavor make this bean dip a favorite. I find that a bottled salsa works best in this recipe because it's not as liquidy as most homemade salsas. If using homemade salsa, drain it well before using.

1½ cups cooked or 1 (15-ounce) can pinto beans, drained and rinsed

½ teaspoon chili powder

1½ cups tomato salsa, well drained

1 cup guacamole

½ cup vegan sour cream

1 (4-ounce) can diced mild green chiles

1 tablespoon fresh lime juice

¼ teaspoon salt

4 green onions, finely chopped

1 ripe tomato, coarsely chopped

½ cup sliced pitted black olives

¼ cup finely chopped fresh cilantro

Tortilla chips, for serving

1. In a medium bowl, mash the beans with the chili powder. Add ½ cup of the salsa and mix well to combine. Spread the bean mixture on the bottom of a glass bowl or in a circular shape on a platter. Spread the guacamole on top, followed by the remaining 1 cup salsa.

2. In a small bowl, combine the sour cream, chiles, lime juice, and salt. Mix well. Spread the sour cream mixture on top of the salsa.

3. In a separate small bowl, combine the green onions, tomato, and olives. Spread the vegetable mixture on top of the sour cream mixture and sprinkle with the cilantro. Cover and refrigerate for at least 30 minutes before serving. This dip is best if eaten on the same day that it is made. Serve with tortilla chips.

seitan buffalo wingz

Okay, so they're not really from Buffalo and they're not really wings (thank goodness)—but they are a hearty and delicious way to enjoy seitan. The sauce recipe is purposely on the mild side to please a wider variety of palates, but if everyone in your crowd likes spicy food, add more hot sauce. Otherwise, you can just serve hot sauce on the side for folks who want to spice things up a bit more. Both the seitan and the sauce can be made up to three days in advance and stored (separately) tightly covered in the refrigerator until needed. They can also be frozen for up to two weeks.

BROTH

6 cups water
1 medium yellow onion, quartered
¼ cup soy sauce
2 garlic cloves, crushed

SEITAN

2 cups vital wheat gluten (wheat gluten flour)
¼ cup nutritional yeast
1 teaspoon paprika
1 teaspoon onion powder
1 teaspoon garlic powder
½ teaspoon salt
½ teaspoon dried thyme
3 tablespoons olive oil
2 cups water

COATING

1 cup plain unsweetened soy milk or other nondairy milk
½ cup yellow cornmeal
2 tablespoons cornstarch
½ teaspoon onion powder
½ teaspoon paprika
½ teaspoon salt
1½ cups panko bread crumbs

SAUCE

½ cup ketchup
3 tablespoons pure maple syrup
2 tablespoons light brown sugar
1 tablespoon spicy brown mustard
1 tablespoon soy sauce
1 tablespoon apple cider vinegar
½ teaspoon hot sauce

1. Make the broth: In a pot, combine the water, onion, soy sauce, and garlic and place it on the stove. Preheat the oven to 400°F. Lightly grease a baking sheet and set aside.

2. Make the seitan: In a large bowl, combine the vital wheat gluten, yeast, paprika, onion powder, garlic powder, salt, and thyme. Add the oil and enough water to make a kneadable dough. Knead for 2 minutes, then use your hands to shape into a 1-inch-thick log. Slice the log into 3-inch pieces and place them in the broth. Bring just to a boil over high heat, then reduce to a simmer and cook, uncovered, for 30 minutes. Drain the seitan and set it aside.

3. Make the coating: Place the soy milk in a shallow bowl. In a separate shallow bowl, combine the cornmeal, cornstarch, and spices, stirring to mix well. In a third shallow bowl, place the panko.

4. Dip the cooked seitan pieces in the soy milk, then dredge them in the cornmeal mixture, then back into the soy milk, and then into the panko. Place the coated seitan pieces on the prepared baking sheet and bake until golden brown, about 15 minutes.

5. Make the sauce: In a small saucepan, combine all the sauce ingredients over medium heat, stirring to blend. Simmer, stirring, until the sauce thickens, about 10 minutes. Spoon the sauce over the baked seitan, then place it back in the oven and bake 5 minutes longer. Serve hot.

make ahead   **quick & easy**

ultimate taco bar

Once you have prepared all the components and arranged them on the table or countertop, the guests take over and make their own customized tacos. All you need to do is refill any ingredients that run low. Another good addition to the taco bar is the Super Slaw (page 146), which is a nice change from the usual lettuce and can also be enjoyed as a side dish. The taco filling can be prepared up to two days in advance and stored in the refrigerator. The toppings (except the avocado) may be prepared in advance and refrigerated until serving time.

$1\frac{1}{2}$ cups cooked or 1 (15.5-ounce) can pinto beans, drained and rinsed

1 tablespoon olive oil

8 ounces seitan or simmered tempeh, finely minced

$\frac{1}{4}$ cup water

1 teaspoon chili powder

1 teaspoon paprika

$\frac{1}{2}$ teaspoon ground cumin

$\frac{1}{2}$ teaspoon salt

$\frac{1}{4}$ teaspoon onion powder

$\frac{1}{4}$ teaspoon garlic powder

$\frac{1}{4}$ teaspoon ground cayenne

$\frac{1}{4}$ teaspoon sugar

$\frac{1}{8}$ teaspoon dried oregano

$\frac{1}{8}$ teaspoon freshly ground black pepper

8 (6-inch) corn tortillas

8 (6-inch) flour tortillas

2 cups tomato salsa

3 cups finely shredded iceberg lettuce

1 cup coarsely chopped fresh ripe tomatoes

$\frac{1}{2}$ cup coarsely chopped red onion

$\frac{1}{2}$ cup coarsely chopped green onion

$\frac{3}{4}$ cup vegan sour cream

$\frac{1}{2}$ cup coarsely chopped pitted black olives

2 ripe Hass avocados

1. In a medium bowl, coarsely mash the beans and set aside. In a large skillet, heat the oil over medium heat. Add the seitan and cook until browned, about 7 minutes. Stir in the mashed beans, water, chili powder, paprika, cumin, salt, onion powder, garlic powder, ground cayenne, sugar, oregano, and pepper and cook, stirring to coat. Keep warm over low heat.

2. Preheat the oven to 300°F. Wrap a stack of corn tortillas in foil. Wrap a separate stack of flour tortillas in foil. Place both stacks of tortillas in the oven to warm, about 10 minutes.

3. In separate bowls, arrange the salsa, lettuce, tomatoes, red onion, green onion, sour cream, and olives. Just before serving, peel and pit the avocados, cut them into ½-inch dice, and place them in a bowl.

4. When ready to serve arrange all of the bowls on a table or countertop along with a bowl containing the warmed seitan and bean mixture and a platter containing the warm tortillas.

make ahead   quick & easy

everyone's favorite ice cream cake

Ice cream cakes are a favorite with kids of all ages, but if you want a vegan one, you'll have to make it yourself. This one uses three different flavors, but you can use any combination of flavors you like. Be sure to prepare the cake well in advance so it has time to refreeze before serving.

1½ cups vegan chocolate cookie crumbs

¼ cup vegan margarine, melted

1 pint vegan chocolate ice cream, softened

1 pint vegan vanilla ice cream, softened

1 pint vegan strawberry ice cream, softened

½ cup crushed unsalted peanuts

Chocolate curls, for garnish

8 whole strawberries, for garnish

Optional garnishes: chocolate sauce, strawberry sauce, vegan whipped cream

1. Lightly grease the bottom and sides of a 9-inch springform pan and set aside. Place the cookie crumbs and the margarine into the pan and stir to moisten the crumbs. Press the crumb mixture into the bottom of the prepared pan and set aside.

2. Transfer the chocolate ice cream into the prepared crust and spread it evenly, smoothing the top with a rubber spatula. Spread the vanilla ice cream in an even layer on top of the chocolate ice cream, followed by the strawberry ice cream, spreading evenly and smoothing the top. Place the cake in the freezer to firm up, at least 4 hours.

3. Remove the cake from the freezer, remove the sides of the springform pan, and cut the cake into 8 slices. Return the cake to the freezer until ready to serve.

4. To serve, sprinkle the peanuts on top of the cake and garnish with chocolate curls and strawberries. Serve with optional garnishes of choice, if using.

make ahead　　**quick & easy**

a tapas table

The popular Spanish custom of enjoying tapas with drinks can be a terrific springboard for a party and a great way to entertain. What's not to like about small plates of tasty appetizers oozing with Mediterranean flavors?

Typical tapas dishes include a wide range of flavors and varied textures and can include very simple dishes as well as more complex ones. If your tapas party is being held in cold weather, consider serving a Spanish sherry and/or a dry red wine. In warmer weather, pitchers of sangria and cold beer can hit the spot.

the menu

TOTALLY TAPAS

Patatas Bravas
Spanish Orange Salad
Sherried Mushrooms
Olive-and-Caper-Stuffed Cherry Tomatoes
Garlic Chickpeas and Spinach

Go-Withs: *toasted bread, roasted almonds, marinated olives, marinated artichoke hearts; sherry, red wine, beer*

recipe swaps

The following recipes could be swapped out for any of the tapas menu recipes or included along with them if you prefer to offer more choices:

Chorizo en Croûte (page 190)
Artichoke-Stuffed Mushrooms (page 260)
Chickpea Artichoke Bites with Rosemary
  Aïoli (page 153)
Artichoke Tapenade (page 38)

patatas bravas

You can find these traditional spicy potatoes on the menu at many tapas bars. A touch of vegan mayonnaise is added to the sauce to mellow the heat and help coat the potatoes with saucy goodness.

1 pound Yukon gold potatoes, peeled and cut into ½-inch dice

2½ teaspoons smoked Spanish paprika

Salt and freshly ground black pepper

1 tablespoon olive oil

2 tablespoons minced yellow onion

1 large garlic clove, minced

2½ tablespoons tomato paste

1 tablespoon red wine vinegar

¾ teaspoon sugar

¼ teaspoon ground cayenne

2½ tablespoons vegan mayonnaise

1 teaspoon hot sauce

2 tablespoons minced fresh parsley

1. Preheat the oven to 400°F. Spread the diced potatoes on a well-greased baking sheet. Sprinkle with 1 teaspoon of the paprika and season with salt and pepper, to taste, tossing to coat. Roast the potatoes until tender and nicely browned, turning once, about 25 minutes.

2. While the potatoes are roasting, make the sauce. In a small saucepan, heat the oil over medium heat. Add the onion, cover, and cook until tender, 3 minutes. Stir in the garlic and cook until fragrant, about 30 seconds. Stir in the tomato paste, vinegar, sugar, cayenne, and the remaining 1½ teaspoons paprika.

3. Remove from the heat, stir in the mayonnaise and hot sauce, and season with salt and pepper, to taste. Mix well and set aside.

4. Combine the potatoes with the sauce and sprinkle with the parsley. Serve warm on small plates.

spanish orange salad

Orange salads are popular throughout the Mediterranean regions and Spain has numerous variations, including one that adds cold diced potatoes. While Valencia oranges are more authentic, I prefer the always sweet, always seedless navel oranges for this dish. You can use either in this refreshing addition to your tapas menu.

3 navel or Valencia oranges, peeled, pith removed, and halved lengthwise

¼ cup finely minced red onion

2 tablespoons toasted slivered almonds

12 cured black olives, halved and pitted

4 fresh mint leaves, rolled and sliced into thin ribbons

2 tablespoons fresh lemon juice

1 tablespoon olive oil

1 teaspoon sugar

Salt and freshly ground black pepper

1. Cut the orange halves crosswise into ¼-inch slices and arrange them on a serving platter.

2. Sprinkle with the onion, almonds, olives, and mint.

3. In a small bowl, whisk together the lemon juice, oil, sugar, and salt and pepper, to taste, and then spoon over the salad.

sherried mushrooms

Spanish sherry and garlic combine to make these mushrooms fragrant and flavorful. They are best served with small slices of warm crusty bread. Adjust the amount of red pepper flakes used according to your own heat tolerance.

1 tablespoon olive oil

8 ounces white mushrooms, lightly rinsed, patted dry, and halved if small, quartered if large

3 to 5 garlic cloves, finely minced

¼ cup dry sherry

1½ tablespoons fresh lemon juice

¼ to ½ teaspoon crushed red pepper

¼ teaspoon smoked Spanish paprika

Salt and freshly ground black pepper

2 tablespoons minced fresh parsley

1. In a large skillet, heat the oil over medium-high heat. Add the mushrooms and cook, stirring, until seared, about 2 minutes.

2. Reduce the heat to medium and add the garlic, sherry, lemon juice, crushed red pepper, paprika, and salt and black pepper, to taste. Cook, stirring, until the garlic and mushrooms are softened, about 5 minutes.

3. Remove from the heat, sprinkle with parsley, and serve hot on small plates.

make ahead   **quick & easy**

olive-and-caper-stuffed cherry tomatoes

MAKES 24 TOMATOES

Your home tapas "bar" should contain a balance of flavors, textures, and temperatures. These flavorful cherry tomatoes, best served at room temperature, are easy to make ahead and require no cooking.

24 cherry tomatoes
⅓ cup vegan cream cheese, at
  room temperature
¼ cup minced pitted kalamata
  olives
¼ cup minced capers
3 tablespoons finely minced
  fresh basil

¼ teaspoon salt
⅛ teaspoon freshly ground black
  pepper
24 fresh parsley leaves, for
  garnish

1. Carefully slice off the top of each tomato. Use a small spoon to scoop out the pulp of each tomato, being careful not to tear the skins. Place the tomato shells upside down on a paper towel to drain out any remaining juice. Set aside.

2. In a medium bowl, combine the cream cheese, olives, capers, basil, salt, and pepper. Mix until well blended.

3. Use a small spoon to fill each tomato with the mixture. Arrange the filled tomatoes on a platter and place a parsley leaf on top of each to garnish. These taste best if made about an hour before serving time and stored at room temperature. However, you can make them up to a day in advance, if necessary, and refrigerate in a tightly covered container. Bring to room temperature before serving.

garlic chickpeas and spinach

MAKES 6 SERVINGS

This dish is so quick and simple to prepare yet loaded with flavor and nutrients. It can be enjoyed "as is" on small plates or spooned onto slices of toasted bread.

2 tablespoons olive oil

3 garlic cloves, minced

3 cups cooked or 2 (15.5-ounce) cans chickpeas, drained and rinsed

½ cup vegetable broth

9 ounces fresh baby spinach

Salt and freshly ground black pepper

1. In a large skillet, heat the oil over medium heat. Add the garlic and cook, stirring, until fragrant and softened, about 2 minutes. Do not brown.

2. Add the chickpeas and broth, stirring to heat through. Crush about half of the chickpeas lightly with a potato masher, then add the spinach and cook, stirring, until just wilted, about 3 minutes. Season with salt and pepper, to taste, and cook until the spinach is further wilted and hot and the flavors have blended, about 5 minutes. Serve immediately.

make ahead   quick & easy

chinese new year

Chinese food is a perennial favorite that makes a welcome meal anytime, but if you're looking for a great excuse to throw a party, consider celebrating Chinese New Year. For this menu I have included enough recipes to make a very special feast. If you make all the menu items, there will be enough food to serve six people, possibly eight. The recipes can, of course, be used selectively for smaller get-togethers. For example, you could omit the Pearl Balls and the Pan-Fried Sesame Noodles and Broccoli and still present a wonderful meal for guests. Of course, any one of the recipes can be enjoyed on its own for everyday meals, and, since quick and easy stir-fries are often the answer to "What's for dinner?" a menu filled with delicious Chinese recipes will no doubt be tapped throughout the year.

the menu

GOOD FORTUNE MENU

Pearl Balls
Hot and Sour Soup
Pan-Fried Sesame Noodles and Broccoli
Brown Rice with Pineapple and Green Onions
Caramelized Tofu
Szechwan Green Beans and Shallots

Go-Withs: orange sorbet garnished with mandarin orange slices, fortune cookies; green tea, Chinese beer

spring festival

Also called the Spring Festival, Chinese New Year occurs soon after the winter solstice, near the end of January through mid-February. It's a great time of year to have a festive party to chase away those winter blahs.

Chinese New Year festivities include many colorful traditions, some of which can be incorporated into your party, if you like. The color red is used for decorating, so now is the time to pull out that red tablecloth and those bowls you have stashed in the closet. Red envelopes containing money are traditionally given to children by the parents. In a spin on that tradition, you could stuff the envelopes for your guests with a small memento of the party—maybe a little chart of the Chinese zodiac.

pearl balls

This unusual and delicious appetizer uses glutinous rice (also called sweet or sticky rice), available at Asian markets. The "pearl" in the name comes from the fact that the rice turns a pearlescent shade when cooked.

½ cup glutinous rice
1 cup firm tofu, drained and crumbled
3 shiitake mushroom caps, lightly rinsed, patted dry, and minced
3 green onions, minced
2 water chestnuts, minced
1 teaspoon grated fresh ginger

2 tablespoons soy sauce, plus more for serving
1 tablespoon dry sherry
1 teaspoon toasted sesame oil
2 tablespoons vital wheat gluten (wheat gluten flour)
1 tablespoon tapioca flour
Salt and freshly ground black pepper

1. Place the rice in a bowl with enough water to cover. Soak overnight. Drain well, then spread the rice on an ungreased baking sheet and set aside.

2. In a large bowl, combine the tofu, mushrooms, green onions, water chestnuts, ginger, soy sauce, sherry, and oil. Sprinkle with the vital wheat gluten, tapioca flour, and salt and pepper, to taste. Mix thoroughly until well combined. Set aside.

3. Pinch off about 1 tablespoon of the mixture and shape it into a ball. Roll it over the glutinous rice so that rice adheres to the ball. Place the pearl ball on a heatproof plate and continue with the remaining ingredients, arranging the balls ½ inch apart. You may need to use more than one plate.

4. Set up a large metal steamer or a bamboo steamer set in a wok. Working in batches if necessary, place a plate containing pearl balls in the steamer basket. Cover and steam over boiling water until they are cooked, about 30 minutes. Serve hot with soy sauce.

hot and sour soup

This Chinese restaurant favorite tastes even better when you make it at home because you can "have it your way"—making it more or less hot or sour according to your own tastes.

3 dried wood ear mushrooms or dried black mushrooms

1 cup fresh shiitake mushroom caps, lightly rinsed, patted dry, and cut into ¼-inch strips

½ cup canned bamboo shoots, drained, rinsed, and cut into matchsticks

1 teaspoon grated fresh ginger

4 ounces seitan, cut into ¼-inch strips

4 ounces firm tofu, drained and cut into ½-inch dice

¾ cup minced green onions

3 tablespoons soy sauce

5 cups light vegetable broth or water

3 tablespoons rice vinegar

1 teaspoon sugar

Salt and freshly ground black pepper

1½ tablespoons cornstarch dissolved in 3 tablespoons water

1 teaspoon sriracha, or to taste

½ teaspoon Asian chili oil

1 teaspoon toasted sesame oil

1. Place the dried mushrooms in a heatproof bowl. Cover with boiling water and set aside until softened, about 20 minutes.

2. Finely slice the softened dried mushrooms and place them in a large pot. Add the shiitake mushrooms, bamboo shoots, and ginger. Add the seitan, tofu, green onions, and soy sauce, then stir in the broth and bring to a boil over high heat. Reduce the heat to low, and simmer, uncovered, for 20 minutes.

3. Add the vinegar, sugar, and salt and pepper, to taste. Blend the cornstarch mixture into the soup, stirring until the soup thickens. Add the sriracha, chili oil, and sesame oil. Taste and adjust the seasonings, if necessary. Serve hot. If not using right away, cool to room temperature, then cover and refrigerate until needed.

make ahead   **quick & easy**

pan-fried sesame noodles and broccoli

MAKES 4 TO 6 SERVINGS

The creamy and flavorful sesame sauce absorbs quickly into the noodles, so if you like your noodles especially saucy, you might want to make a little extra sauce to add when ready to serve. Chinese sesame paste is made from toasted sesame seeds and has a distinctly different flavor from the Middle Eastern sesame tahini. Look for Chinese sesame paste in Asian markets or online.

12 ounces linguine or egg-free Chinese noodles

1 tablespoon toasted sesame oil

⅓ cup Chinese sesame paste

¼ cup soy sauce

1 tablespoon rice vinegar

1 teaspoon sriracha, or to taste

1 teaspoon light brown sugar

½ cup vegetable broth or water

1 tablespoon neutral vegetable oil

3 green onions, minced

1½ teaspoons grated fresh ginger

3 cups small broccoli florets, lightly steamed

1 tablespoon toasted sesame seeds, for garnish

1. In a large pot of boiling salted water, cook the linguine over medium-high heat, stirring occasionally, until al dente, about 10 minutes. (If using Chinese noodles, cook according to package directions.) Drain the noodles well, rinse, and place them in a large bowl. Toss with the sesame oil and set aside.

2. In a small bowl, combine the sesame paste, soy sauce, vinegar, sriracha, sugar, and broth and mix until well blended. Set aside.

3. In a large skillet or wok, heat the vegetable oil over medium-high heat. Add the green onions and ginger and cook until fragrant, about 30 seconds. Add the broccoli and the cooked noodles. Stir in the sesame sauce and toss gently to combine until hot. Transfer to a large serving bowl and sprinkle with the sesame seeds. Serve hot.

brown rice with pineapple and green onions

Green onions, ginger, crushed red pepper, and chopped pineapple combine with rice for a dish that's a little spicy, a little sweet, and a lot delicious. It's also a very pretty dish that transforms rice from side dish to sensational.

2 tablespoons neutral vegetable oil

1 large bunch green onions, minced

2 teaspoons grated fresh ginger

½ teaspoon crushed red pepper

2 teaspoons light brown sugar

3 tablespoons soy sauce

4 cups cooked brown rice

1½ cups finely chopped fresh or canned pineapple

Salt and freshly ground black pepper

1. In a large skillet, heat the oil over medium-high heat, add the green onions and ginger and cook until softened, about 1 minute.

2. Add the crushed red pepper, sugar, soy sauce, and rice, stirring to mix evenly. Stir in the pineapple and season with salt and black pepper, to taste. Cook, stirring occasionally, to heat through, about 7 minutes. Serve hot or warm. If not using right away, cover and refrigerate until needed, then reheat.

make ahead   **quick & easy**

caramelized tofu

This is probably one of the simplest ways to prepare tofu and it's also one of the most flavorful. Nicely browned and slightly sweet, this dish is a great way to introduce tofu to the uninitiated. The tofu can be cooked in advance, and other ingredients chopped ahead of time, but the dish itself is so quick to prepare, it's best done at the last minute.

1 pound extra-firm tofu, cut into ¼-inch slices and pressed
Salt and freshly ground black pepper
2 tablespoons neutral vegetable oil
2 medium shallots, cut into ½-inch slices
3 green onions, minced
2 cloves garlic, minced
2 tablespoons light brown sugar
¼ cup coarsely chopped fresh cilantro leaves

1. Pat the tofu dry and season with salt and pepper, to taste.

2. In a large skillet, heat the oil over medium heat. Add the tofu, in batches if necessary, and cook until golden brown on both sides, about 4 minutes per side. Remove the tofu from the skillet and set aside.

3. Add the shallots, green onions, and garlic to the pan and cook for 1 to 2 minutes to soften. Add the sugar, stirring to dissolve. Return the tofu to the pan and cook for about 5 minutes to heat through, turning to coat. Add the cilantro and serve hot.

szechwan green beans and shallots

Spicy and crisp-tender, these green beans are as flavorful as any you'd find in a Chinese restaurant, but they're better for you because they're stir-fried in only 1 tablespoon of oil instead of the larger amounts used in restaurants.

1 pound green beans, trimmed

2 tablespoons soy sauce

1 teaspoon grated fresh ginger

1 tablespoon dry sherry

2 teaspoons Asian chili paste

1 teaspoon cornstarch

1 teaspoon toasted sesame oil

1 tablespoon neutral vegetable oil

3 medium shallots, minced

1 small red bell pepper, cut into ¼-inch strips

1 garlic clove, minced

Salt and freshly ground black pepper

1. Steam the green beans until just tender, about 6 minutes. Rinse under cold water and set aside.

2. In a small bowl, combine the soy sauce, ginger, sherry, chili paste, cornstarch, and sesame oil. Set aside.

3. In a large skillet or wok, heat the vegetable oil over medium-high heat. Add the shallots and bell pepper and stir-fry until softened, about 2 minutes. Add the garlic and stir-fry 30 seconds longer. Add the green beans, then add the sauce to the skillet. Season with salt and black pepper, to taste. Cook, stirring, until the sauce comes to a boil. Continue cooking and stirring until the beans are coated, 2 minutes. Serve hot.

make ahead   quick & easy

curry
for
company

With its bold complex flavors and exotic aromas, an Indian meal can be a transporting experience that can be enjoyed any time of year, including the Hindu holidays of Holi, the festival of colors, which is celebrated sometime in early spring, and Diwali, the festival of lights, observed in early autumn.

Use brightly colored table linens and dinnerware, as well as a centerpiece of fresh fruit, flowers, and candles that matches the festive mood of this menu. Play a CD of Indian music softly in the background.

The components of this menu can be made in advance, so there's no last-minute kitchen work if company's coming.

the menu

AN INDIAN FEAST

Curried Pakora Puffs
Mixed Vegetable Curry
Spinach-Flecked Chapati
Mango-Mint Chutney
Coconut Basmati Rice with Cashews
Cardamom Rice Pudding

Go-Withs: *mango lassi*

recipe swaps

Rice Dish: *Instead of making the coconut rice, serve plain basmati rice.*

Dessert: *Try the Coconut Snowballs (page 67)*

last-minute rescues

To save time, instead of making the Curried Pakora Puffs, thaw a sheet of puff pastry and cut it into ½-inch strips. Sprinkle with a curry spice blend and rub it into the pastry so it sticks. Pick up a pastry strip with both hands and twist each end in opposite directions to make a twisted pastry stick. Place the pastry twist on a baking sheet and repeat with the remaining pastry. Bake at 400°F until golden brown, about 10 minutes.

If you don't have time to make your own chutney, buy a jar of prepared chutney.

curried pakora puffs

These bite-size puffs have all the flavor of pakoras without the fuss. They're easy to make and can be prepared ahead of time — just pop in the oven to bake or reheat when needed. No sauce is needed, although a bowl of chutney or minted vegan yogurt makes a nice accompaniment.

1 pound white potatoes, peeled and cut into ½-inch dice

1 tablespoon neutral vegetable oil

1 medium yellow onion, minced

1 serrano or other hot green chile, seeded and minced

1 teaspoon grated fresh ginger

2 cups finely chopped fresh spinach

2 teaspoons hot or mild curry powder

1 teaspoon salt

½ teaspoon ground coriander

¼ teaspoon freshly ground black pepper

2 tablespoons plain unsweetened soy milk or other nondairy milk

3 tablespoons minced fresh cilantro

3 tablespoons chickpea flour

½ teaspoon baking powder

1. Steam the potatoes until tender, about 15 minutes. Transfer to a bowl and set aside.

2. In a large skillet, heat the oil over medium heat. Add the onion, cover, and cook until softened, 5 minutes. Uncover, add the chile, ginger, and spinach and cook for 2 minutes. Preheat the oven to 375°F. Lightly grease a baking sheet or line it with parchment paper or a silicone mat. Set aside.

3. Sprinkle the steamed potatoes with the curry powder, salt, coriander, and pepper. Add the soy milk and mash well. Stir in the onion mixture, then add the cilantro, flour, and baking powder. Mix well to combine.

4. Use your hands to shape about 1 tablespoonful of the mixture into a 1-inch ball. Place it on the prepared baking sheet and repeat with the remaining mixture until it is all used up. Bake until lightly browned, about 30 minutes. Serve hot.

mixed vegetable curry

A variety of colorful vegetables are bathed in a luscious curry sauce. Serve over the Coconut Basmati Rice with Cashews or plain cooked basmati rice, if you prefer.

1 tablespoon neutral vegetable oil

1 large yellow onion, coarsely chopped

2 medium carrots, cut into ¼-inch slices

2 garlic cloves, minced

1 jalapeño or other fresh hot chile, seeded and minced

1 teaspoon grated fresh ginger

1 tablespoon hot or mild curry powder

¾ teaspoon ground coriander

½ teaspoon ground cumin

1 (13.5-ounce) can unsweetened coconut milk

4 ounces green beans, trimmed and cut into 1-inch pieces

2½ cups (1-inch) cauliflower florets

½ teaspoon salt

⅛ teaspoon freshly ground black pepper

1½ cups cooked or 1 (15.5-ounce) can dark red kidney beans, drained and rinsed

1 cup frozen peas, thawed

1. In a large saucepan, heat the oil over medium heat. Add the onion and carrots. Cover and cook until softened, 5 minutes. Add the garlic, chile, and ginger. Cook, stirring until softened, about 1 minute.

2. Stir in the curry powder, coriander, and cumin, then add the coconut milk, green beans, and cauliflower. Add the salt and pepper. Cover and simmer until the vegetables are softened, about 15 minutes.

3. Stir in the kidney beans and peas, and simmer, uncovered, for 10 minutes to heat through and blend the flavors. Taste and adjust the seasonings, if necessary. Serve hot. If not using right away, transfer to a bowl and cool to room temperature, then cover and refrigerate for up to 3 days and reheat when ready to serve.

make ahead   **quick & easy**

spinach-flecked chapati

MAKES 8 CHAPATI

You can use fresh or frozen spinach, but make sure it is squeezed very dry before chopping. Chapati are unleavened Indian flatbreads made with whole wheat flour. Tender and soft when freshly made, chapati are best if eaten right away.

1 cup whole wheat flour
1 cup all-purpose flour
1 teaspoon salt
¾ cup cooked spinach, squeezed
  dry and coarsely chopped

1 tablespoon neutral vegetable
  oil, plus more for frying
¾ cup warm water
2 tablespoons vegan margarine,
  melted

1. In a large bowl, combine the whole wheat flour, all-purpose flour, and salt. Mix well, then add the spinach, oil, and water and mix well to form a soft dough.

2. Knead the dough until smooth, about 3 minutes. Cover tightly with plastic wrap and let the dough rest for 30 minutes.

3. Preheat the oven to 200°F. Divide the dough into 8 equal pieces. Roll out each piece of dough on a lightly floured work surface into ⅛-inch-thick rounds.

4. In a griddle or large skillet, heat a thin layer of oil over medium heat. Add the chapati, one at a time, and cook, turning once, until golden brown on both sides, about 4 minutes per side.

5. Transfer the cooked chapati to a heatproof platter and brush with the melted margarine. Cover loosely with foil and keep warm in the oven while you cook the remaining chapati. Serve immediately.

mango-mint chutney

MAKES ABOUT 2 CUPS

This colorful, fresh-tasting chutney is an ideal complement to this meal. If you prefer a less chunky chutney, you can blend a portion of it in the food processor once it has cooled to room temperature and then stir it back in.

¼ cup minced shallot
1 tablespoon grated fresh ginger
⅓ cup golden raisins
⅓ cup sugar
⅓ cup water
3 tablespoons apple cider vinegar
¼ teaspoon crushed red pepper

¼ teaspoon salt
2 to 3 ripe medium mangoes, peeled, pitted, and coarsely chopped
¼ cup coarsely chopped fresh mint leaves

1. In a large saucepan, combine the shallot, ginger, raisins, sugar, water, vinegar, crushed red pepper, and salt and bring to a boil over medium heat. Reduce the heat to low and simmer, stirring occasionally, for 5 minutes.

2. Add the mangoes and cook, stirring frequently, to blend the flavors, about 15 minutes. Cool to room temperature. Stir in the mint. If not using right away, spoon the chutney into a container with a tight-fitting lid. Cover and refrigerate until needed. Properly stored, this chutney will keep for up to 1 week.

make ahead   **quick & easy**

coconut basmati rice with cashews

Made with coconut milk and garnished with cashews and cilantro, this rice dish is loaded with flavor and texture.

1 tablespoon neutral
  vegetable oil
½ cup finely minced yellow
  onion
1½ cups basmati rice
1 (13-ounce) can unsweetened
  coconut milk

1¼ cups water
1 tablespoon sugar (optional)
½ teaspoon salt
½ cup crushed unsalted roasted
  cashews
2 tablespoons minced fresh
  cilantro

1. In a medium saucepan, heat the oil over medium heat. Add the onion, cover, and cook until softened, about 5 minutes.

2. Uncover and stir in the rice, then add the coconut milk and water and bring just to a boil over high heat. Reduce the heat to medium and stir in the sugar, if using, and the salt. Cover and simmer until the rice is tender, 40 to 45 minutes. If the liquid evaporates before the rice is tender, stir in a small amount of additional water and cover and cook until tender. Cover and set aside to allow flavors to blend, about 5 minutes.

3. Serve hot, sprinkled with the cashews and cilantro. If not using right away, reserve the garnish and cover and refrigerate until needed, up to 2 days. When ready to serve, reheat the rice and garnish with the cashews and cilantro.

cardamom rice pudding

Cardamom lends its distinctive flavor to this creamy rice pudding. The optional pistachios add color and crunch.

3 cups cooked basmati rice
1½ cups plain or vanilla soy
  milk or other nondairy milk
⅓ to ½ cup sugar
¼ teaspoon ground cardamom

1 teaspoon pure vanilla extract
1 teaspoon coconut extract
¼ cup crushed unsalted
  pistachios (optional)

1. In a medium saucepan, combine the rice, soy milk, and sugar and bring to a boil over high heat. Reduce the heat to medium and simmer, uncovered, stirring frequently, until the rice is creamy, about 20 minutes.

2. Stir in the cardamom and continue to cook until the pudding has thickened, 5 to 10 minutes longer. Remove from the heat, stir in the vanilla and coconut extracts, and set aside to cool to room temperature.

3. Spoon the pudding into dessert bowls, then cover and refrigerate for 1 hour or longer to chill. Serve sprinkled with pistachios, if using.

make ahead   quick & easy

holiday
gatherings

a super bowl party

There's no need to wait for the actual Super Bowl to throw this party, as you can certainly make a "super bowl" of chili anytime with the Devil's Details Chili recipe. This casual menu is also ideal to serve while watching other sporting events, such as basketball, soccer, or the Olympics. It can also be made when you have the neighbors over to play cards or for an impromptu supper with friends. Best of all, these recipes can be made in advance (in fact, the chili and slaw taste even better when made a day or more ahead).

These are very hearty dishes (some might call it "guy food"), so feel free to modify the menu, depending on how many people you're having over and what kind of eaters they are. For example, you can eliminate the dip and the tempeh fingers, and just put out chips and salsa as a prelude to the chili, slaw, and cornbread muffins. These recipes serve four to six and can be easily doubled for a larger crowd.

Because of its casual nature, this menu works best served as a buffet. Simply put everything on a sideboard, countertop, or table, along with plates and utensils, and let guests serve themselves. Use a Crock-Pot to serve the chili and keep it warm. Depending on the occasion or how much room you have, you can direct your guests to eat their food at a dining table or to "sit anywhere" (around the coffee table in the living room, for example) and enjoy.

the menu

SUPER CHILI BOWL

Olive-cado Dip

Finger-Lickin' Tempeh Fingers

Super Slaw

Devil's Details Chili

Confetti Corn Muffins

Man-Size Chocolate Chip Cookies

Go-Withs: *chips, salsa; beer and more beer*

recipe swaps

Dip: *Vegetable Dippers with Ranch Dressing* (page 210)

Appetizer: *Spinach-Potato Quesadillas* (page 189)

Main Dish: *Black Bean and Butternut Chili* (page 224)

Dessert: *Chocolate Lover's Brownies* (page 92)

olive-cado dip

MAKES ABOUT 3 CUPS

The piquant flavor of green olives combines with creamy avocados for a tasty variation on guacamole. Serve with your favorite chips.

3 ripe Hass avocados, pitted, peeled and cut into ½-inch dice

Juice of 1 lime

½ cup pitted green olives, finely chopped

1 serrano chile, seeded and minced

3 tablespoons minced red onion

3 tablespoons minced fresh cilantro

Salt and freshly ground black pepper

⅓ cup pitted kalamata olives, chopped, for garnish

1. Place the avocados in a medium bowl. Add the lime juice and mash with a fork.

2. Add the green olives, serrano, onion, cilantro, and salt and pepper, to taste. Stir gently to combine. Garnish with kalamata olives. Serve immediately.

last-minute rescues

Even if you've doubled up on your dip and chili and made a huge batch of slaw, you may still find your guests with the munchies over the course of an evening. Here are two easy solutions:

Extra salsa and chips: If your dip runs low, fill in with salsa and chips. You can also keep a few extra ripe avocados on hand to whip up a batch of guacamole.

Extra dessert: A plate of large chocolate chip cookies makes a great casual dessert. Trouble is, nobody can eat just one—or two. Consider making a double batch to keep as a backup. If you don't end up needing them for the party, they freeze well.

finger-lickin' tempeh fingers

The spicy-sweet sauce made with smoky chipotles and apple juice cooks into the tempeh as it simmers, making these luscious "fingers" finger-lickin' good.

16 ounces tempeh

2 garlic cloves, minced

2 tablespoons tomato paste

2 teaspoons minced chipotle chile in adobo

⅔ cup apple juice

¼ cup soy sauce

2 tablespoons pure maple syrup

2 tablespoons apple cider vinegar

1 teaspoon ground cumin

1 teaspoon ground coriander

2 tablespoons olive oil

1. Cut the tempeh into ½-inch bars. In a medium saucepan of simmering water, cook the tempeh over medium heat for 20 minutes. Drain and set aside.

2. In a bowl, combine the garlic, tomato paste, chipotle, apple juice, soy sauce, maple syrup, vinegar, cumin, and coriander. Mix together and set aside.

3. In a large skillet, heat the oil over medium-high heat. Add the tempeh and cook until golden brown on both sides, turning once, about 5 minutes per side. Pour the sauce mixture over the tempeh, reduce the heat to medium, and simmer, uncovered. About halfway through, turn the tempeh and spoon the sauce over the tempeh. Simmer until the sauce reduces and becomes syrupy, about 10 minutes.

4. Serve hot drizzled with any remaining sauce. If not using right away, the tempeh fingers can be refrigerated for up to 3 days and reheated when needed.

make ahead   **quick & easy**

super slaw

This crunchy and colorful coleslaw is great anytime, but it's really super when served on Super Bowl Sunday.

½ head green cabbage, shredded (about 6 cups)

⅓ small head red cabbage, shredded (about 2 cups)

2 large carrots, shredded

3 small radishes, shredded

¼ cup minced red onion

¼ cup sherry vinegar

1½ teaspoons sugar

1 teaspoon Dijon mustard

½ teaspoon celery seed

1 teaspoon salt

¼ teaspoon freshly ground black pepper

¼ cup olive oil

1. In a large bowl, combine the green and red cabbages, carrots, radishes, and onion. Set aside.

2. In a small bowl, combine the vinegar, sugar, mustard, celery seed, salt, and pepper, stirring to blend and dissolve the sugar and salt. Stir in the oil, mixing until well blended.

3. Add the dressing to the slaw, stirring to coat. Cover and refrigerate for at least 1 hour before serving, to allow flavors to blend. Properly stored in the refrigerator, the slaw will keep well for several hours or overnight.

make ahead   **quick & easy**

party**vegan**

devil's details chili

MAKES 4 TO 6 SERVINGS

They say the devil is in the details and this spicy chili has some devilish details. The black coffee, chipotle chile, and unsweetened cocoa, give depth to the flavor and balance the acidity of the tomatoes. Like most chilis, this one benefits from being made a day or two in advance and refrigerated, then reheated when ready to serve. It also freezes well for up to two weeks.

1 tablespoon olive oil

1 large yellow onion, finely chopped

1 medium carrot, minced

3 garlic cloves, minced

8 ounces shredded seitan

3 tablespoons chili powder

1½ tablespoons unsweetened cocoa powder

1½ teaspoons ground cumin

1 teaspoon smoked paprika

1 teaspoon dried marjoram

1 teaspoon sugar

1 teaspoon salt

¼ teaspoon freshly ground black pepper

1 (28-ounce) can crushed tomatoes

1 minced chipotle chile in adobo

3 cups cooked or 2 (15.5-ounce) cans black beans, drained and rinsed

1½ cups cooked or 1 (15.5-ounce) can dark red kidney beans, drained and rinsed

1 (4-ounce) can mild or hot diced green chiles, drained

1¼ cups water

¾ cup strong coffee

¼ cup unsalted pumpkin seeds

1. In a large pot, heat the oil over medium heat. Add the onion and carrot. Cover and cook until softened, about 10 minutes. Uncover and stir in the garlic and seitan. Cook, stirring, for 5 minutes. Stir in the chili powder, cocoa, cumin, paprika, marjoram, sugar, salt, and pepper. Add the tomatoes, chipotle, beans, green chiles, water, and coffee and bring to a boil.

2. Reduce the heat to low and simmer, partially covered, stirring occasionally, until the chili thickens and flavors develop, about 45 minutes. Add a little more liquid if the chili becomes too thick. Serve sprinkled with the pumpkin seeds.

confetti corn muffins

MAKES 1 DOZEN

Nothing beats the combination of chili and cornbread, but serving cornbread at a party can be a "crumby" experience. The solution is to make corn muffins instead. These muffins are studded with colorful bits of corn, chiles, and cilantro, making them not only extra-flavorful, but all dressed up for a party.

1 cup all-purpose flour

1 cup yellow cornmeal

2 teaspoons baking powder

1 teaspoon salt

1 cup plain soy milk or other nondairy milk

⅓ cup olive oil

2 tablespoons pure maple syrup

½ cup fresh or thawed frozen corn kernels

¼ cup finely minced red bell pepper

¼ cup canned mild or hot green chiles, drained and minced

¼ cup minced fresh cilantro

1 teaspoon minced chipotle chile in adobo

1. Preheat the oven to 375°F. Lightly grease a 12-cup muffin tin or line with paper liners and set aside.

2. In a large bowl, combine the flour, cornmeal, baking powder, and salt and set aside.

3. In a separate large bowl, combine the soy milk, oil, maple syrup, corn, bell pepper, green chiles, cilantro, and chipotle.

4. Add the wet ingredients to the dry ingredients and mix well with a few quick strokes.

5. Transfer the batter to the prepared pan and bake until golden brown and a toothpick inserted in the center comes out clean, about 25 minutes. Cool 10 minutes on a wire rack. Serve warm or at room temperature. If not using right away, cool completely then cover and store at room temperature until needed. These muffins taste best if eaten on the same day that they are made, but can be made several hours ahead and reheated, if desired.

man-size chocolate chip cookies

After Tami Noyes tested these cookies, she prefaced her comments by telling me that she's particularly picky about chocolate chip cookies. Fortunately, these cookies passed her test with flying colors: she reported that they have just the right texture—slightly crispy on the outside and a wee bit of softness inside.

¾ cup vegan margarine, softened

¾ cup light brown sugar

¼ cup granulated sugar

¼ cup plain or vanilla soy milk or other nondairy milk

3 tablespoons pure maple syrup

1 teaspoon pure vanilla extract

1¼ cups all-purpose flour

1 cup whole wheat pastry flour

1 teaspoon baking soda

½ teaspoon baking powder

½ teaspoon salt

1 cup vegan semisweet chocolate chips

¾ cup coarsely chopped walnuts or pecans (optional)

1. Preheat the oven to 350°F. Line 2 baking sheets with parchment paper or silicone mats.

2. In a large bowl, cream together the margarine and both sugars until light and fluffy. Stir in the soy milk, maple syrup, and vanilla and mix until smooth.

3. In a separate large bowl, combine both flours, baking soda, baking powder, and salt and mix well. Add the dry ingredients to the wet ingredients, stirring well to combine. Fold in the chocolate chips and walnuts, if using.

4. Drop the dough by the heaping tablespoonful (or more) about 2 inches apart onto the prepared baking sheets. Bake until slightly browned around the edges, 15 to 16 minutes. Cool for a few minutes on the sheet before transferring to a wire rack to cool. When completely cool, store in an airtight container for up to 2 days.

make ahead **quick & easy**

be my valentine dinner for two

Unlike most of the menus in this book, which serve four people or more, this special Valentine's Day dinner is designed for two. It's a romantic menu filled with heart-shaped surprises for you and your special someone. The dinner is certainly not just for February 14—if you simply omit the heart shapes, you'll have a wonderful meal for any special occasion, whether it's a first date or your silver anniversary. In fact, these recipes are too good not to share and can be easily doubled to make a special dinner for four and more.

This menu is a little more elaborate than most of the others in this book and consists of multiple courses, including an appetizer and a soup. If you decide to omit the first two courses, the rest of the meal will still be spectacular, so use your judgment regarding your comfort level and plan accordingly.

For the table setting, decide if you want to go all out with a heart-shaped theme or keep it simple and sophisticated. In either case, candlelight and the "good china" are definitely in order. Break out the cloth napkins, too, and consider some soft background music to capture the mood.

the menu

A PAIR OF HEARTS

Chickpea-Artichoke Bites with Rosemary Aïoli
Red Bliss Potato and Fennel Soup
Pastry-Wrapped Seitan Roulades with Spinach-
  Mushroom Duxelles
Heart-Beet Rösti
Sautéed Rainbow Chard with Balsamic Drizzle
Chocolate-Cherry Cheesecake

Go-Withs: *champagne or your favorite wine, coffee*

recipe swaps

Appetizer: *Artichoke Tapenade (page 38)*
Soup: *If you prefer a salad, try the Mixed Greens*
    with Caramelized Walnuts and Balsamic-Pear
    Vinaigrette (page 240)
Main Dish: *Quinoa-Stuffed Portobello Mushrooms*
    with Wine-Braised Shallots (page 251)
Dessert: *Chocolate "Pots de Crème" (page 204)*

how to avoid a valentine's day massacre

This particular menu isn't the easiest one in the book. After all, you're trying to impress that special someone. If preparing the entire menu is beyond your comfort level, here are some modifications to ensure that your special meal is stress-free. The following suggestions can also come in handy as substitutions for particular items or in case you run out of time to prepare everything on the menu:

No time to make appetizer or soup? No worries—the first two courses can be omitted and you'll still have a delicious meal.

The adorable and delicious beet rösti are well worth the time and trouble, but for an easy alternative pick up a package of presteamed baby beets (look for them in the produce section of upscale grocers such as Trader Joe's). Just slice and add to the chard sauté for that splash of red that says "It's Valentine's Day."

No time to make cheesecake? Keep a quart of vegan vanilla ice cream in the freezer and transform a simple scoop into a sophisticated and delicious dessert special enough to serve on Valentine's Day: scoop the ice cream into pretty dessert dishes or barware such as martini or wine glasses. Drizzle with chocolate sauce or your favorite liqueur and garnish with a strawberry or a few raspberries.

chickpea-artichoke bites with rosemary aïoli

MAKES ABOUT 12 PUFFS

These sophisticated nibbles are easy to make and can be prepared ahead of time. The accompanying aïoli adds luscious layers of extra flavor, although these tasty bites can also be enjoyed on their own.

1 small russet potato, peeled and cut into ½-inch dice (about ½ cup)

½ cup cooked or canned chickpeas, drained and rinsed

¾ cup finely chopped canned (unmarinated) or cooked frozen artichoke hearts

1 tablespoon minced fresh parsley

1½ teaspoons olive oil

1½ teaspoons fresh lemon juice

2 teaspoons nutritional yeast

¼ teaspoon Dijon mustard

¼ teaspoon garlic powder

½ teaspoon salt

⅛ teaspoon freshly ground black pepper

1½ tablespoons chickpea flour

½ teaspoon baking powder

Rosemary Aïoli (recipe follows)

1. Steam the potato until tender, about 15 minutes. Preheat the oven to 400°F. Lightly grease a baking sheet or line with parchment paper or a silicone mat. Set aside.

2. In a medium bowl, mash the chickpeas. Add the cooked potato and mash together. Add the artichoke hearts, parsley, oil, juice, yeast, mustard, garlic powder, salt, pepper, flour, and baking powder. Mix well to combine.

3. Pinch off a small amount of the mixture and use your hands to roll it into a 1-inch ball. Place it on the prepared baking sheet. Repeat until all the mixture is used up.

4. Bake for about 18 minutes, then turn the puffs over and bake until lightly browned, about 10 minutes longer. Arrange on a platter with a small bowl of the aïoli and serve warm. If not serving right away, they can be covered and refrigerated for up to 2 days or frozen for up to 2 weeks and then reheated when needed.

make ahead   **quick & easy**

rosemary aïoli

1 garlic clove, crushed
1 teaspoon minced fresh
  rosemary
¼ teaspoon salt

1½ teaspoons fresh lemon juice
1½ teaspoons sherry vinegar
½ teaspoon Dijon mustard
⅓ cup vegan mayonnaise

1. In a food processor, combine the garlic, rosemary, and salt and process until well minced. Add the remaining ingredients and process until well blended. Taste and adjust the seasonings, if necessary.

2. Scrape the aïoli into a small bowl. Cover and refrigerate until needed. The aïoli can be made up to a day in advance.

red bliss potato and fennel soup

Pronounced "lovely and delicious" by recipe testers Jenna and Russell Patton, this luxurious soup is sure to win the hearts of those near and dear any time of year. But when it's made with potatoes named Red Bliss, it deserves to be served on Valentine's Day. If Red Bliss potatoes are unavailable, Yukon golds are a good substitute, despite their lack of romantic moniker. Either way, potatoes paired with fennel make an ideal couple in this creamy soup. The fennel makes this soup lighter in texture than you would expect from a potato soup, and the slight anise flavor of tarragon complements the flavor of the fennel.

1 tablespoon olive oil

1 large shallot, coarsely chopped

2 cups vegetable broth

6 ounces Red Bliss potatoes, unpeeled, scrubbed, and cut into ½-inch dice

1 small fennel bulb, chopped, reserving a few fronds

½ cup plain unsweetened soy milk or other nondairy milk

Salt and freshly ground black pepper

2 teaspoons minced fresh tarragon or fennel fronds

1. In large saucepan, heat the oil over medium heat. Add the shallot, cover, and cook until softened, about 5 minutes. Add the broth, potatoes, and fennel bulb. Bring to a boil. Reduce the heat to low and simmer, uncovered, until the potatoes are soft, about 20 minutes.

2. Transfer the potato mixture to a blender or food processor. Puree until smooth. Return the soup to the pot. Stir in the soy milk and season with salt and pepper, to taste. Simmer to heat through and blend flavors, about 5 minutes. Ladle the soup into bowls and sprinkle with tarragon. Serve hot.

155

make ahead   **quick & easy**

pastry-wrapped seitan roulades with spinach-mushroom duxelles

MAKES 2 SERVINGS

Although this recipe involves a few steps, it can be assembled ahead of time and the delicious results are well worth the effort.

SEITAN

½ cup vital wheat gluten (wheat gluten flour)

2 teaspoons nutritional yeast

¼ teaspoon onion powder

⅛ teaspoon salt

3 tablespoons soy sauce

2 tablespoons olive oil

½ cup cold water

DUXELLES

1 tablespoon olive oil

⅓ cup minced yellow onion

2 cups finely chopped white mushrooms

2 cups fresh spinach leaves, coarsely chopped

2 teaspoons soy sauce

2 teaspoons dry white wine

½ teaspoon dried thyme

¼ teaspoon dried sage

¼ teaspoon salt

⅛ teaspoon freshly ground black pepper

1 sheet vegan puff pastry, thawed

1. Make the seitan: In a large bowl, combine the vital wheat gluten, yeast, onion powder, and salt. Stir to mix well. Add 1 tablespoon of the soy sauce,1 tablespoon of the oil, and the water and stir until well mixed. Turn the mixture out onto a lightly floured work surface and divide it in half. Stretch one of the pieces into a flat rectangle, then place it between two sheets of plastic wrap or parchment paper. Let it rest for 5 minutes, then use a rolling pin to flatten it as much as you can (it will be elastic and resistant). Repeat with the remaining piece. Top them with a baking sheet weighed down with canned goods for 10 minutes and set aside.

2. In a large skillet, heat the remaining 1 tablespoon of oil over medium heat. Add the seitan and cook until golden brown on both sides, turning once, about 4 minutes per side. Pour enough water into the skillet to cover

156

the seitan and add the remaining 2 tablespoons soy sauce. Bring just to a boil, then reduce heat to low and simmer, uncovered, for 45 minutes. Remove the seitan from the water and set aside to cool.

3. Make the duxelles: In a separate large skillet, heat the oil over medium heat. Add the onion, cover, and cook until softened, 5 minutes. Stir in the mushrooms, spinach, soy sauce, wine, thyme, sage, salt, and pepper. Cook, stirring, until the spinach is wilted and the mushrooms release their juice, about 4 minutes. Continue cooking until the liquid from the mushrooms evaporates and the duxelle mixture is nearly dry, about 5 minutes. Remove from the heat and set aside to cool.

4. Place the pastry sheet on a lightly floured work surface and divide into thirds, reserving one third for another use. Roll out the remaining 2 pieces of pastry with a floured rolling pin.

5. Place one of the seitan cutlets in the center of each piece of pastry. Spoon a mound of the duxelle mixture in the center of each piece of seitan and roll up the seitan to enclose the stuffing. Then gently wrap the pastry around the seitan to enclose it. Moisten the edges with water, if needed, to help seal the pastry around the seitan. Refrigerate for 30 minutes or until ready to serve. If not serving right away, cover tightly and refrigerate for up to 24 hours.

6. Preheat the oven to 400°F. Place the pastry-wrapped roulades on an ungreased baking sheet, seam side down, and bake until the pastry is golden brown, about 25 minutes. Serve hot.

make ahead   quick & easy

heart-beet rösti

MAKES 2 SERVINGS

Shredded beets and potato are molded into a heart shape for Valentine's Day and baked until tender on the inside and crisp on the outside. Tip: To remove the skin from the beets, place them in a saucepan of boiling water for about 5 minutes, then plunge them into cold water. This should loosen the skins enough to remove easily.

1 large red beet, peeled
1 medium white potato, peeled
¼ cup grated yellow onion
¼ cup all-purpose flour
¼ teaspoon salt

⅛ teaspoon freshly ground black pepper
2 tablespoons olive oil
Minced fresh parsley or chives, for garnish

1. Preheat the oven to 375°F. Generously grease a small heart-shaped cake pan or a large baking sheet. Grate the beet and potato in a food processor. (You can grate them by hand, but it will be messy.) Place the grated beet, potato, and onion in a medium bowl. Sprinkle with the flour, salt, and pepper and toss well to coat.

2. If using the heart-shaped pan, spread the beet and potato mixture in the pan and press with a spatula to compress evenly. If you don't have a heart-shaped pan, transfer the mixture to the prepared baking sheet and press it together inot the shape of a heart. (You can divide the mixture in half and shape it into 2 smaller hearts, if you prefer.) Drizzle with the oil, cover tightly with foil, and bake for 20 minutes.

3. Carefully remove the rösti from the oven and place a plate on top, invert, and slide the rösti (even if baked in the pan) onto the baking sheet. If you've made small hearts, flip them over carefully with a metal spatula. Return to the oven to brown the other side, about 20 minutes. Garnish with parsley and serve hot. If not serving right away, allow the rösti to come to room temperature, then cover and refrigerate until needed, then reheat. Although the rösti can be made several hours ahead, they're best if used on the same day they are made.

make ahead   **quick & easy**

sautéed rainbow chard with balsamic drizzle

MAKES 2 SERVINGS

Colorful and delicious, rainbow chard sautéed with shallots, pine nuts, and golden raisins makes an easy and elegant side dish for this romantic meal. A drizzle of balsamic syrup at the end adds a wonderful flavor note.

¼ cup balsamic vinegar
1½ teaspoons sugar
1 tablespoon olive oil
1 medium shallot, thinly sliced
1½ tablespoons pine nuts
1 bunch rainbow chard, cut crosswise into ½-inch strips (4 to 5 cups)

2 tablespoons water
1½ tablespoons golden raisins
¼ teaspoon salt
⅛ teaspoon freshly ground black pepper

1. In a small saucepan, combine the vinegar and sugar and bring to a boil over high heat. Reduce the heat to low and cook until the vinegar reduces by half, about 5 minutes. Set aside.

2. In a large skillet, heat the oil over medium heat. Add the shallot and cook until it begins to soften, about 2 minutes. Add the pine nuts and cook, stirring, until lightly toasted, about 3 minutes.

3. Add the chard and cook, stirring, until wilted, about 3 minutes. Add the water and cook, covered, until tender, about 3 minutes. Uncover, add the raisins, salt, and pepper and continue to cook until the water evaporates, about 2 minutes more. Serve hot, drizzled with the balsamic syrup. Store any unused syrup covered in the refrigerator for another use. It will keep for several days.

159

chocolate-cherry cheesecake

This decadent dessert is a perfect ending to a special meal. If you're making this cake for Valentine's Day, fresh cherries may be hard to find. Substitute raspberries or strawberries, if available, or use frozen fruit or canned pie filling.

1 cup vegan chocolate cookie crumbs

3 tablespoons vegan margarine, melted

⅔ cup vegan semisweet chocolate chips

2 (8-ounce) containers vegan cream cheese, at room temperature

¾ cup sugar

¼ cup plain or vanilla soy milk or other nondairy milk

1 teaspoon pure vanilla extract

½ cup cherry jam

12 fresh ripe cherries, pitted

¼ cup sliced almonds, toasted

1. Preheat the oven to 350°F. Lightly grease the bottom and sides of a 7-inch springform pan and set aside. Place the cookie crumbs in the prepared pan and drizzle in as much of the margarine as needed to moisten the crumbs, mixing with a fork to combine. Press the crumb mixture into bottom and sides of pan, and set aside.

2. Melt the chocolate chips in a double boiler or microwave and keep warm.

3. In a food processor, combine the cream cheese, sugar, soy milk, and vanilla, and blend until smooth. Add the chocolate and blend until smooth. Scrape the batter into the prepared crust and spread evenly. Bake until firm, about 40 minutes.

4. Turn off the oven and let the cake remain in the oven for 15 minutes. Remove the cake from the oven and cool on a wire rack. Refrigerate several hours to chill completely. The cheesecake may be made 1 to 2 days in advance if stored tightly covered in the refrigerator.

5. When ready to serve, place the jam in a small bowl and stir briskly until smooth. Spread the jam thinly over the top of the cheesecake. Arrange the cherries on top around the outer edge and sprinkle the almonds in the center.

make ahead   **quick & easy**

st. patrick's day menu

On St. Patrick's Day in years past, I had to restrain myself from adding green food coloring to everything I cooked. Thankfully, I've mellowed since those days, so this menu focuses on the foods and flavors of Ireland, and includes a judicious number of naturally green dishes (no food coloring in sight!). The recipes in this menu can also be enjoyed anytime you want to get your Irish up—no need to reserve them for March 17 alone.

As far as decorations and tableware, this is one of the holidays where it's easy (and fun) being green. Use a green tablecloth and napkins and green or white dishes. A live shamrock plant (or a group of them) makes a lovely centerpiece. If you're into paper shamrocks and other such decorations, now's your chance to go wild.

As with many of the menus in this book, this one provides recipes to allow you the flexibility of serving multiple courses at a seated dinner or a variety of dishes on a buffet. For a simpler meal, you could omit either the soup or the salad, or both, and simply serve the Irish stew accompanied by the soda bread for a hearty meal anytime.

the menu

POTLUCK OF THE IRISH
Pea Green Soup
Whiskey and Soda Bread
Shamrock Vegetable Salad
Colcannon-Topped Irish Stew
Creamy Lime-Pistachio Parfaits

Go-Withs: lots of beer (green food coloring optional)

recipe swaps

Soup: *Artichoke Tapenade (page 38)*

Side Dish: *Baby Greens with Lemony Vinaigrette
    (page 250)*

last-minute rescues

*Here are a few "rescue remedies" and substitutions to help keep your
dinner party stress-free:*

Steada Soda Bread: *If you don't have time to bake soda bread, serve a
loaf of crusty French or Italian bread.*

Keep It Green: *Instead of making the shamrock salad, steam green
beans or broccoli and serve with a vinaigrette. Even easier, serve a
simple lettuce salad.*

Pass on the Parfaits: *For a shortcut dessert, scoop up lime sorbet, vegan pistachio ice cream, or basic vanilla served in pretty dessert dishes or
martini or wine glasses and drizzle with a bit of green crème de menthe,
Midori, or other green liqueur. Or top with crushed pistachios or some
diced kiwifruit for that touch of green.*

pea green soup

The delicate flavors of sweet peas and leaf lettuce merge deliciously in this creamy soup. For a garnish, I like the crunch of pistachios and the green-on-green color, but you can opt for chopped kalamata olives, chopped tempeh bacon, or shamrock-shaped croutons instead.

1 tablespoon olive oil
2 large shallots, coarsely chopped
3 cups coarsely chopped leaf lettuce
3 cups frozen peas
4 cups vegetable broth

Salt and freshly ground black pepper
¾ cup plain unsweetened soy milk or other nondairy milk
2 tablespoons shelled unsalted pistachios, for garnish

1. In a large pot, heat the oil over medium heat. Add the shallots, cover, and cook until softened, about 5 minutes. Uncover, add the lettuce, and cook until wilted, about 3 minutes. Stir in the peas and broth and season with salt and pepper, to taste. Bring to a boil, then reduce the heat to low and simmer, uncovered, for 20 minutes.

2. Transfer the soup to a blender or food processor and process until smooth, in batches if necessary, and return to the pot. Stir in the soy milk and taste and adjust the seasonings, if necessary. Reheat over low heat until hot, about 3 minutes. If not using right away, the soup may be cooled to room temperature and refrigerated for up to 2 days, then heated when ready to serve.

3. Ladle into bowls, sprinkle with pistachios, and serve hot.

make ahead   **quick & easy**

whiskey and soda bread

MAKES 4 SMALL LOAVES

Steeping the raisins in whiskey and shaping the bread into individual loaves add fun twists to this St. Paddy's day favorite.

¼ cup whiskey

½ cup golden raisins

1¼ cups warm plain soy milk or other nondairy milk

2 teaspoons apple cider vinegar

4 cups all-purpose flour

¼ cup sugar

1½ teaspoons salt

1½ teaspoons baking powder

1 teaspoon baking soda

1. Preheat the oven to 375°F. Lightly grease a baking sheet and set aside. In a small saucepan, bring the whiskey just to a boil over high heat. Remove from the heat and add the raisins. Set aside to let the raisins steep.

2. In a small bowl, combine the soy milk and vinegar and set aside.

3. In a large bowl, combine the flour, sugar, salt, baking powder, and baking soda. Mix until blended. Mix in the soy milk mixture and the steeped raisins, stirring to make a soft dough.

4. Turn the dough out onto a lightly floured work surface and knead for 1 minute, then divide into quarters. Shape each quarter into a small round loaf and arrange the loaves on the prepared baking sheet. Flatten the loaves slightly with your hands and use a sharp knife to cut an X-shaped slash into the top of the loaves.

5. Bake until golden and a toothpick inserted in the center comes out clean, about 30 minutes. Cool on a wire rack for 10 minutes before serving. These loaves can be made several hours ahead, but are best if eaten on the same day they are baked.

shamrock vegetable salad

This verdant salad is proof that there can't be too much green on St. Patrick's Day.

2 cups lightly blanched broccoli florets

1 cup lightly blanched snow peas, cut into 1-inch pieces

½ green bell pepper, cut into matchsticks

½ cucumber, peeled, seeded, and coarsely chopped

1 ripe Hass avocado, pitted, peeled, and cut into ½-inch dice

½ cup pitted green olives, halved

½ cup thawed frozen green peas

¼ cup olive oil

2 tablespoons fresh lemon juice

½ teaspoon sugar

½ teaspoon salt

⅛ teaspoon freshly ground black pepper

1. In a large bowl, combine the broccoli, snow peas, bell pepper, cucumber, avocado, olives, and peas. Set aside.

2. In a small bowl, combine the oil, lemon juice, sugar, salt, and black pepper. Blend well and pour the dressing over the vegetables. Toss gently to combine. Serve immediately.

make ahead   **quick & easy**

colcannon-topped irish stew

MAKES 6 SERVINGS

Irish classics colcannon and Irish stew (made with seitan) team up to create a hearty shepherd's pie–style casserole that can be assembled several hours in advance and refrigerated, then baked when you're ready for dinner.

STEW

1 tablespoon olive oil

1 yellow onion, coarsely chopped

2 garlic cloves, minced

2 large carrots, cut into ¼-inch slices

2 cups kale, coarsely chopped

12 ounces seitan, cut into ½-inch dice

2 cups vegetable broth

¼ cup dry white wine, optional

2 tablespoons soy sauce

1 teaspoon dried thyme

Salt and freshly ground black pepper

8 ounces white mushrooms, lightly rinsed, patted dry, and cut into ½-inch slices

1 cup frozen peas

2 tablespoons minced fresh parsley

COLCANNON

3 russet potatoes, peeled and cut into 2-inch chunks

2 cups finely chopped kale

¼ cup plain unsweetened soy milk or other nondairy milk

3 tablespoons vegan margarine

½ teaspoon salt

¼ teaspoon freshly ground black pepper

3 tablespoons all-purpose flour

1. Make the stew: In a large pot, heat the oil over medium heat. Add the onion, cover, and cook until softened, about 5 minutes. Add the garlic and carrots and cook, stirring, 3 minutes more.

2. Add the kale and seitan. Pour in the broth, wine, if using, soy sauce, thyme, and salt and pepper, to taste. Bring to a boil over high heat, then reduce the heat to low, cover, and simmer until the vegetables are tender, about 30 minutes. Uncover, stir in the mushrooms, peas, and parsley, and cook for 10 minutes longer. Taste and adjust seasonings, if necessary. Set aside.

3. Make the colcannon: While the stew is simmering, cook the potatoes in a pot of boiling salted water until tender, about 20 minutes. During the last 10 minutes of cooking time, stir in the kale.

4. Drain well and transfer the potatoes and kale to a large bowl. Mash the potatoes slightly, then add the soy milk, 1 tablespoon of the margarine, and salt and pepper, to taste. Mash until smooth.

5. Preheat the oven to 350°F. Use a slotted spoon to transfer the stew into a 9 x 13-inch baking pan, reserving the liquid.

6. In a small saucepan, melt the remaining 2 tablespoons margarine over medium heat. Add the flour and cook, stirring, until blended. Add the liquid from the stew, stirring until thickened. Taste and adjust seasonings, adding more thyme or tamari, if necessary. Pour the sauce over the stew.

7. Spread the colcannon evenly on the top of the stew. Bake until hot, about 45 minutes. Serve hot.

make ahead   **quick & easy**

My single favorite ingredient for impressive and easy appetizers (and desserts) is as close as your supermarket freezer case— Pepperidge Farm puff pastry. It's delicious, versatile, easy to use, and best of all—it's vegan. Puff pastry can be used to make all sorts of sweet and savory delights. When making a number of small hors d'oeuvres, you can assemble them in advance, freeze them on baking sheets, and then, once frozen, store them in zip-top freezer bags. When needed, they can go from freezer to baking sheet and into the oven to bake up crisp and fresh for serving.

You can cut and shape puff pastry into triangles, palmiers, twists, crescents, puffs, pillows, and tarts. You can fill them to make miniature versions of empanadas or samosas, spanakopita triangles, or tiny calzones. Puff pastry can be wrapped around olives, stuffed mushrooms, or small chiles for a burst of flavor "en croûte." You can also make zesty "straws" by cutting the pastry into strips, twisting, and sprinkling with vegan Parmesan or a variety of herbs and seasonings. Puff pastry can be used to work dessert magic, too: just assemble your favorite combination of sugar, spices, nuts, chocolate, or fruit and you can make tarts, turnovers, napoleons, palmiers, and even profiteroles.

creamy lime-pistachio parfaits

MAKES 4 TO 6 SERVINGS

Layers of pistachio-cashew crème alternate with layers of lime-avocado puree to make pretty green-on-green parfaits that are an ideal way to end a St. Patrick's Day meal. This dessert can be made several hours in advance but is best if eaten on the same day that it is made.

1 cup shelled unsalted pistachios
½ cup unsalted raw cashews
1 cup sugar
½ cup plain or vanilla soy milk or other nondairy milk

2 teaspoons pure vanilla extract
2 ripe Hass avocados, pitted, peeled, and coarsely chopped
¾ cup firm silken tofu, drained
3 tablespoons fresh lime juice
Fresh mint leaves, for garnish

1. In a high-speed blender, combine ½ cup of the pistachios and the cashews and grind to a powder. Add ½ cup of the sugar, the soy milk, and 1 teaspoon of the vanilla. Blend until smooth and creamy. Transfer to a small bowl and set aside.

2. In a blender or food processor, combine the avocados, tofu, the remaining ½ cup sugar, lime juice, and the remaining 1 teaspoon vanilla and process until smooth. Set aside.

3. Crush the remaining ½ cup of pistachios. To assemble, spoon a layer of crushed pistachios into the bottom of 4 parfait or wineglasses. Add a layer of the avocado mixture, followed by a layer of the pistachio crème, followed by another layer of the avocado mixture. Cover and refrigerate for 30 minutes to 1 hour or up to several hours.

4. When ready to serve, top with the remaining pistachios and garnish with mint leaves.

make ahead   **quick & easy**

phat tuesday party

In New Orleans, Mardi Gras is celebrated on the Tuesday before Lent begins (*mardi gras* means "fat Tuesday" in French), usually around the end of February. However, I think any time is a good time to throw a Mardi Gras party.

Decorate your house and table in green, purple, and gold. Make it a costume party and display masks. Serve absinthe in Pontarlier glasses, dust off your zydeco CDs, and put out the spread in this chapter.

The menu combines the country bayou Cajun traditions with more sophisticated Creole city food, all with my own interpretations. Whether it's Mardi Gras or not, these dishes are guaranteed to "let the good times roll."

the menu

LAISSEZ LES BON TEMPS ROULEZ!

Collard and Red Bean Fritters
Rémoulade Sauce
Smoke and Spice Jambalaya
Grits 'n' Greens
Pastry-Wrapped Bananas Foster

Go-Withs: Cajun-spiced popcorn; hurricanes, beer,
wine, or punch

last-minute rescue

*If you're phyllo-phobic, skip the pastry part of the dessert
and simply sauté the bananas and pecans in the margarine, brown sugar, and rum and spoon it over the vegan
vanilla ice cream.*

collard and red bean fritters

This will make about 12 good-size (two-bite) fritters. If serving as pickup food, you can make them a bit smaller, if desired. Serve these tasty fritters with rémoulade sauce (see below). For extra crunch, coat the fritters in panko instead of cornmeal or regular bread crumbs.

1 cup cooked or canned dark red kidney beans, rinsed and drained

1½ cups finely chopped cooked collard greens

¼ cup minced green onion

2 garlic cloves, minced

1 teaspoon Cajun seasoning

½ teaspoon salt

¼ teaspoon freshly ground black pepper

¾ cup coarse yellow cornmeal or dried bread crumbs

½ cup plain unsweetened soy milk or other nondairy milk

Olive oil, for frying

Rémoulade Sauce (recipe follows)

1. Place the beans in a large bowl and mash well. Add the collard greens, green onion, garlic, Cajun seasoning, salt, and pepper. Add ¼ cup of the cornmeal and mix thoroughly until well combined. Shape the mixture into 1½-inch fritters and refrigerate for 20 minutes.

2. Place the soy milk in a shallow bowl. Place the remaining ½ cup cornmeal in a shallow bowl. Dip the chilled fritters in the soy milk, then dredge them in the cornmeal.

3. In a large skillet, heat a thin layer of oil over medium heat. Add the fritters and fry them until golden brown, turning frequently. Serve hot with the rémoulade sauce. If not using right away, the fritters may be covered and refrigerated for up to 2 days or frozen for up to 2 weeks, then reheated when ready to serve.

make ahead   **quick & easy**

rémoulade sauce

MAKES ABOUT ¾ CUP

½ cup vegan mayonnaise

1 tablespoon minced green onion

1 tablespoon minced fresh parsley

1½ tablespoons ketchup

1 tablespoon capers, drained and coarsely chopped

1 teaspoon spicy brown mustard

1 teaspoon minced fresh tarragon or ½ teaspoon dried

1 teaspoon Tabasco sauce

½ teaspoon smoked paprika

¼ teaspoon salt

In a small bowl, combine all the ingredients. Stir to mix well. Cover and refrigerate for 30 minutes before serving to allow flavors to blend. If not using right away, cover tightly and store in the refrigerator for up to 3 days.

smoke and spice jambalaya

In Louisiana, there are about as many versions of jambalaya as there are cooks, so let's add this vegan version to the group. Instead of seitan or tempeh, you can add cooked red beans or sliced and sautéed vegan sausage. If not everyone in your crowd likes it spicy, you can leave out the chipotles and put the bottle of Tabasco on the table for folks to add on their own.

8 ounces tempeh

2 tablespoons olive oil

8 ounces seitan, cut into
  ½-inch dice

1 medium yellow onion,
  coarsely chopped

2 celery ribs, coarsely chopped

1 medium green bell pepper,
  coarsely chopped

3 garlic cloves, minced

1 (28-ounce) can fire-roasted
  diced tomatoes, drained

1 cup long-grain rice

2 chipotle chiles in adobo,
  minced

3 cups vegetable broth

1 teaspoon smoked paprika

1 teaspoon dried marjoram

1 teaspoon salt

¼ teaspoon freshly ground black
  pepper

1 tablespoon coarsely chopped
  fresh parsley, for garnish

Tabasco sauce, for serving

1. In a medium saucepan of simmering water, cook the tempeh over medium heat for 30 minutes. Drain, pat dry, and cut into ½-inch dice.

2. In a large pot, heat 1 tablespoon of the oil over medium heat. Add the tempeh and seitan and cook until browned, stirring occasionally, about 8 minutes. Remove from the pot and set aside.

3. Heat the remaining 1 tablespoon oil in the same pot. Add the onion, celery, bell pepper, and garlic. Cover and cook until softened, about 7 minutes.

4. Stir in the tomatoes, rice, chipotle, broth, paprika, marjoram, salt, and black pepper. Bring to a boil, then reduce heat to low, cover, and simmer until the rice and vegetables are tender, about 45 minutes. Stir the tempeh and seitan back into the pot and cook 5 minutes longer.

5. To serve, ladle into shallow bowls, sprinkle with parsley and a splash of Tabasco. Serve hot.

grits 'n' greens

This tasty casserole combines two Southern favorites: collard greens and grits. If collards are unavailable, use another dark leafy green such as kale. If grits are unavailable, use coarse-ground polenta cornmeal.

Variation: Add some finely chopped vegan bacon or sausage to the grits when adding the collards and sprinkle the top with shredded vegan cheese.

2 tablespoons olive oil
½ cup finely chopped yellow
  onion
2 garlic cloves, minced
1½ cups cooked collards or
  other greens, finely chopped

Salt and freshly ground black
  pepper
3½ cups vegetable broth
1 cup quick-cooking grits

1. Preheat the oven to 375°F. Lightly grease a 9-inch square baking pan and set aside.

2. In a large skillet, heat the oil over medium heat. Add the onion, cover, and cook until softened, 5 minutes. Uncover, add the garlic, and cook, stirring, for 1 minute. Stir in the collards and season with salt and pepper, to taste. Remove from the heat and set aside.

3. In a large saucepan, bring the broth to a boil over high heat. Add salt to taste (depending on the saltiness of your broth) and stir in the grits. Reduce the heat to low and cook, stirring occasionally, until thickened but not stiff. Remove from the heat and stir in the collard mixture.

4. Spread the mixture evenly into the prepared baking pan. Bake until golden brown, about 30 minutes. Serve hot. If not using right away, the unbaked mixture may be covered and refrigerated for up to 2 days, then baked when ready to serve.

make ahead   **quick & easy**

pastry-wrapped bananas foster

The classic New Orleans dessert, bananas Foster, is given a sophisticated twist. The bananas can be assembled ahead of time and then baked when needed. The sauce can be made in advance, too, and reheated at serving time. Prescoop the ice cream and return it to the freezer, and this showstopping dessert can be plated and served almost effortlessly.

4 sheets phyllo dough
¼ cup vegan margarine, melted
4 ripe medium bananas
2 tablespoons finely ground
   toasted pecans

3 tablespoons light brown sugar
⅓ cup toasted pecan pieces
3 tablespoons dark rum
4 scoops vegan vanilla ice
   cream

1. Preheat the oven to 400°F. Line a baking sheet with parchment paper or a silicone mat and set aside.

2. Brush a sheet of the pastry lightly with the margarine and fold it in half. Place a banana at the bottom end of the folded pastry sheet. Sprinkle the banana with one-fourth of the ground pecans and 1 teaspoon of the sugar. Fold the sides of the pastry over the banana and roll it up tightly. Place the wrapped banana on the prepared baking sheet. Repeat with the remaining bananas. Reserve the remaining margarine. Bake the pastry-wrapped bananas until the phyllo is golden brown, about 18 minutes.

3. While the bananas are baking, heat the remaining margarine in a small saucepan over medium heat. Add the pecan pieces and the remaining sugar and cook, stirring, to dissolve the sugar, about 3 minutes. Add the rum and cook for 2 minutes longer. Keep warm until the bananas have finished baking.

4. To serve, cut the bananas in half on an angle and arrange on dessert plates with ice cream and pecan sauce. Serve immediately.

Note: *Tightly wrap the leftover phyllo pastry and refrigerate or freeze for another use. It will keep for up to 2 weeks in the refrigerator or several months in the freezer.*

make ahead   **quick & easy**

likes and dislikes... and allergies, too

When the guests are people that you know well, then the menu you choose can be informed by their particular likes and dislikes. For example, maybe you know of a favorite dessert or pasta dish to include in your menu. However, when your guests are casual acquaintances or friends you haven't seen in a while, you'll want to choose a menu with a more broad appeal. If you can, try to ascertain whether your guests have any extreme dislikes for any ingredients and find out if they have any food allergies.

Years ago, I spent a full day preparing a lovely meal that featured seitan, only to discover that one of my guests was allergic to gluten. Another time, the menu featured cilantro—an herb for which one guest had a strong aversion. By learning the hard way, I always ask ahead about food preferences in advance. I inquire about food favorites, too. After all, if you're investing the time, money, and effort in having a party, you want your guests not merely to survive it, but to enjoy it. If that means simply avoiding green bell peppers or preparing a chocolate dessert, then such a small preliminary effort will reap satisfying rewards.

passover

During Passover, Jews commemorate the Exodus from Egypt through the seder service and meal. For the seder service, celebrants read the Passover Haggadah aloud and they partake of certain foods symbolic of the Exodus story. For example, tradition holds that the flight from Egypt was so swift, there was no time to wait for the bread to rise. Hence, the use of unleavened matzo at the seder. Other symbolic foods are salt water, a bitter herb, horseradish, haroset (a fruit and nut mixture), a hardboiled egg, and a charred lamb shank bone.

Because some elements of the seder present conflicts for Jewish vegans, many substitute an oval-shaped boiled potato for the egg and a roasted beet for the lamb shank. Here is my interpretation of a vegan seder meal.

the menu

SEDER MENU
Cousin Jenny's Matzo Ball Soup
Roasted Eggplant and Potato Torta
Lemon-Scented Asparagus Bundles
Apple-Pecan Haroset
Fruit Crisp with Matzo Crumb Topping

Go-Withs: red wine, kosher grape juice

recipe swaps

Main Dish: Buttercup Squash Stuffed with Wild Rice,
     Shiitake Mushrooms, and Caramelized Leeks (page 231)

Side Dish: Tarragon Green Beans with Toasted Pine Nuts
     (page 253)

Dessert: Fresh Fruit Picks with Two Dips (page 99);
     Strawberries Dipped in Chocolate (page 71); or
     Pistachio-Dusted Chocolate-Raspberry Truffles (page 96)

cousin jenny's matzo ball soup

MAKES 4 TO 6 SERVINGS

My Italian cousin Louie from Chicago married Jenny, who was Jewish and a fabulous cook. When I was a child, they visited my family regularly and Jenny would head right for the kitchen. Often, she'd make us a pot of her delicious matzo ball soup that I would crave until her next visit. After going vegan, I adapted her recipe so I can still enjoy this comfort food favorite.

MATZO BALLS

1 cup matzo meal

1 tablespoon nutritional yeast

1 tablespoon potato starch

½ teaspoon onion powder

¼ teaspoon garlic powder

1 teaspoon salt

¼ teaspoon freshly ground black pepper

8 ounces firm tofu, well drained and crumbled

¼ cup water

3 tablespoons olive oil

2 tablespoons minced fresh parsley

SOUP

2 tablespoons olive oil

1 medium yellow onion, finely chopped

2 medium carrots, cut into ¼-inch slices

2 celery ribs, cut into ¼-inch slices

3 garlic cloves, minced

7 cups vegetable broth

2 tablespoons minced fresh parsley

1 tablespoon minced fresh dill weed or 1 teaspoon dried

½ teaspoon salt

¼ teaspoon freshly ground black pepper

1. Make the matzo balls: In a medium bowl, combine the matzo meal, yeast, potato starch, onion powder, garlic powder, salt, and pepper. Set aside.

2. In a food processor, combine the tofu, water, oil, and parsley. Process until smooth.

3. Add the tofu mixture to the matzo mixture and mix until well blended. Cover the bowl and refrigerate for 4 hours or overnight.

180

4. Make the soup: In a large pot, heat the oil over medium heat. Add the onion, carrots, and celery. Cover and cook until softened, about 5 minutes. Add the garlic and cook 2 minutes longer. Stir in the broth, parsley, dill weed, salt, and pepper. Bring to a boil, then reduce the heat to low and simmer, uncovered, until the vegetables are just tender, about 20 minutes. Taste and adjust the seasonings, if necessary.

5. Divide the matzo ball mixture into 12 equal portions. Use your hands to shape the mixture into tightly packed balls. Add the matzo balls to the soup, cover, and simmer for 30 minutes, then turn off the heat and set aside for 15 minutes. Serve hot. If not using right away, cool to room temperature, then cover and refrigerate for up to 2 days and reheat when ready to serve.

make ahead   **quick & easy**

roasted eggplant and potato torta

This hearty and flavorful torta makes a great main dish for Passover, or any time you're having guests for dinner. It can be assembled and partially baked ahead of time.

1½ pounds Yukon gold potatoes, peeled and cut into ¼-inch slices

4 tablespoons olive oil

Salt and freshly ground black pepper

2 medium eggplants, cut into ¼-inch slices

1 large yellow onion, minced

1 medium red bell pepper, minced

3 garlic cloves, minced

1 bunch Swiss chard, finely chopped

8 ounces white mushrooms, lightly rinsed, patted dry, and coarsely chopped

1 teaspoon minced fresh thyme

1 (14.5-ounce) can fire-roasted diced tomatoes, drained

3 tablespoons matzo meal

1 tablespoon nutritional yeast

1. Preheat the oven to 400°F. Lightly grease a 3-quart round casserole dish and set aside. Lightly grease 2 large baking sheets.

2. Arrange the potato slices on one of the prepared baking sheets. Drizzle with 1 tablespoon of the oil and season with salt and black pepper, to taste. Bake until the potatoes are softened and golden brown, turning once, about 15 minutes. Arrange the eggplant slices on the second prepared baking sheet. Drizzle with 1 tablespoon of the oil and season with salt and black pepper, to taste. Bake until the eggplant slices are softened and slightly browned, turning once, about 12 minutes. Set aside.

3. In a large skillet, heat 1 tablespoon of the oil over medium heat. Add the onion, cover, and cook until softened, about 5 minutes. Add the bell pepper, garlic, chard, mushrooms, and thyme. Cover and cook until softened, about 5 minutes. Add the tomatoes and season with salt and black pepper, to taste. Uncover and cook, stirring occasionally, until the vegetables are soft and the liquid evaporates, about 7 minutes. Set aside.

4. Arrange a layer of slightly overlapping eggplant slices in the bottom of the prepared casserole. Spread a layer of the vegetable mixture on top of the eggplant. Top with a layer of potatoes, followed by more vegetable mixture, and another layer of eggplant. Repeat until all the ingredients are used. Bake for 30 minutes. If not using right away the torta can be made ahead to this point, then cooled to room temperature, covered, and refrigerated for several hours. Return to room temperature before proceeding with the final baking.

5. In a small bowl, combine the matzo meal, nutritional yeast, and the remaining 1 tablespoon oil, stirring to blend. Sprinkle the mixture on top of the torta and return to the oven for 10 to 15 minutes. Serve immediately

make ahead   **quick & easy**

lemon-scented asparagus bundles

MAKES 4 TO 6 SERVINGS

Since Passover usually occurs when the first asparagus of spring is becoming plentiful, it makes a great choice for a side dish for this meal. The lemon adds a refreshing touch.

1 pound thin asparagus, tough ends trimmed

2 tablespoons olive oil

Salt and freshly ground black pepper

2 to 3 green onions

2 tablespoon fresh lemon juice

2 teaspoons lemon zest

1. Preheat the oven to 425°F. Lightly grease a baking sheet.

2. Arrange the asparagus in a single layer on the prepared baking sheet. Drizzle with the oil and season with salt and pepper, to taste. Roast until the asparagus is just tender, about 8 minutes. Remove from the oven and set aside until cool enough to handle.

3. Trim the white part off the green onions and reserve them for another use. Steam the long green part of the green onions for about 30 seconds, just long enough to make pliable.

4. Divide the asparagus into 4 to 6 small bundles and arrange each bundle in the center of one of the green onion "ribbons." Carefully tie each asparagus bundle with its green onion ribbon. Carefully place the bundles back onto the baking sheet and return to the oven until hot and nicely roasted, about 3 to 4 minutes more.

5. To serve, arrange the bundles on a serving platter and sprinkle with the juice and zest. Serve immediately.

apple-pecan haroset

At the seder, haroset symbolizes the mortar used by the Israelites to build cities for the Pharaoh during their enslavement in Egypt. This flavorful relish also makes a delicious accompaniment for other meals as well, and it is a nice alternative to cranberry sauce at Thanksgiving. It's a little on the sweet side (especially if your apples are sweet), so use a smidge less sugar if you prefer it less so.

½ cup golden raisins

3 tablespoons warm apple juice

1 tablespoon light brown sugar

2 Gala or Fuji apples, peeled, cored, and coarsely chopped

½ cup coarsely chopped pecans

1 teaspoon ground cinnamon

1. In a small bowl, combine the raisins, apple juice, and sugar and soak for 1 hour.

2. Transfer the raisin mixture to a food processor. Add the apples, pecans, and cinnamon and pulse to combine. Do not overprocess since you want the texture to remain slightly chunky. Transfer to a small bowl. Serve immediately or cover and refrigerate until needed. Properly stored, it will keep for up to 2 days.

185

make ahead   **quick & easy**

fruit crisp with matzo crumb topping

This fruit crisp is an ideal dessert to serve during Passover. You can vary the type of fruit used according to your personal preference.

3 crisp baking apples, such as Granny Smith or Macintosh, peeled, cored, and cut into ¼-inch slices
¼ cup pure maple syrup
¾ cup light brown sugar
4 tablespoons water
1½ teaspoons ground cinnamon
¼ teaspoon ground ginger

2 teaspoons fresh lemon juice
1 tablespoon arrowroot powder
3 ripe pears, peeled, cored, and cut into ¼-inch slices
½ cup matzo meal
⅓ cup kosher old-fashioned oats
Pinch salt
5 tablespoons neutral vegetable oil

1. Preheat the oven to 375°F. Lightly grease a 9-inch square baking pan and set aside. In a medium saucepan, combine the apples, maple syrup, ½ cup sugar, 3 tablespoons of the water, 1 teaspoon of the cinnamon, and the ginger. Cover and cook over medium heat until the apples are softened, about 5 minutes.

2. In a small bowl, combine the remaining 1 tablespoon water with the lemon juice and arrowroot powder, stirring to blend. Stir the arrowroot mixture into the apples and remove from the heat. Add the pear slices, mix gently, and spoon the fruit mixture into the prepared baking pan. Set aside.

3. In medium bowl, combine the matzo meal, oats, salt, oil, the remaining ¼ cup sugar, and the remaining ½ teaspoon of cinnamon. Use a pastry blender or fork to mix until crumbly.

4. Sprinkle the topping over the fruit mixture and bake until the top is browned and bubbly, about 20 minutes. Serve warm. If not using right away, cool to room temperature, then cover and refrigerate for up to 2 days. Return to room temperature before serving and warm in the oven if desired.

186

make ahead   quick & easy

cinco
de mayo
celebration

With the popularity of Mexican food in the United States, this Cinco de Mayo menu is one you'll want to enjoy year round. It makes an especially good casual meal to serve when having friends over.

Like many of the menus in this book, this one contains recipes that can be added or deleted to suit the type of gathering and the number of people. If you're serving a crowd, you'd probably want to make all the recipes in the menu and arrange them on a buffet table. If you're just having a few friends over for drinks and snacks, you could, instead, make only Spinach-Potato Quesadillas or the Chorizo en Croûte (or both). Add plenty of chips and salsa, maybe some guacamole, and you've got it covered.

the menu

CINCO DE MAYO AND BEYOND

Spinach-Potato Quesadillas
Chorizo en Croûte
Seitan Enchiladas with Mole Poblano
Romaine and Avocado Salad with
  Cilantro-Cumin Vinaigrette
Tres Leches Cupcakes

Go-Withs: chips, salsa; Mexican beer, margaritas

recipe swaps

Appetizer: Mini Blue Corn Pancakes with Chipotle-
  Streaked Sour Cream (page 216) or Five-Story Bean Dip
  (page 111)

Main Dish: Devil's Details Chili (page 147)

Salad: Super Slaw (page 146)

Dessert: Italian Wedding Cookies (page 69) or
  Pistachio-Dusted Chocolate-Raspberry Truffles (page 96)
  Note: For this party, add a dash of cinnamon and chili
  powder and dust them with crushed pepitas (pumpkin
  seeds) instead of pistachios.

spinach-potato quesadillas

MAKES 4 QUESADILLAS

No cheese in these quesadillas—the yummy potato and spinach filling is all that is needed to hold them together. Chipotle chile adds a touch of heat and corn kernels add a bit of sweetness.

6 garlic cloves

2 tablespoons olive oil

1 pound Yukon gold potatoes, peeled and cut into 1-inch dice

1 teaspoon minced chipotle chile in adobo

Salt and freshly ground black pepper

1 medium red onion, minced

4 cups chopped fresh spinach

4 (10-inch) flour tortillas

1 cup fresh or frozen corn

¼ cup chopped fresh cilantro

Tomato salsa, for serving

1. Preheat the oven to 400°F. Place the garlic on a sheet of foil and drizzle with 1 tablespoon of the oil. Roast the garlic until soft, about 15 minutes. Set aside to cool. Peel and mash and set aside.

2. Place the potatoes in a large saucepan with enough salted water to cover. Bring to a boil and cook until tender, about 20 minutes. Drain and transfer to a large bowl. Add the roasted garlic and chipotle, and season with salt and pepper, to taste. Mash well and set aside.

3. In a large skillet, heat the remaining 1 tablespoon oil over medium heat. Add the onion, cover, and cook until softened, about 5 minutes. Add the spinach and cook until wilted, about 2 minutes.

4. Spread one-quarter of the potato mixture over the surface of 1 tortilla. Spread one-quarter of the onion-spinach mixture on one-half of the potato mixture and top with one-quarter of the corn and cilantro. Fold the tortilla in half to enclose the filling. Repeat with the remaining ingredients.

5. Place the quesadillas in a skillet and cook, one or two at a time, depending on the size of your skillet, until heated through and slightly browned on both sides. Serve with salsa. The quesadillas may be assembled in advance and refrigerated until needed, then reheated.

make ahead   **quick & easy**

chorizo en croûte

MAKES ABOUT 24

Because you're making your own chorizo for these tasty little appetizer bites, the recipe is done in two steps. Even so, they're easy to make and can be prepared ahead of time for a hearty no-fuss appetizer. Come party time, just pop in the oven and serve.

1 cup vital wheat gluten (wheat gluten flour)

3 tablespoons tapioca flour

2 tablespoons nutritional yeast

3 teaspoons chili powder

3 teaspoons garlic powder

2 teaspoons smoked paprika

1 teaspoon dried oregano

1 teaspoon ground cumin

1 teaspoon ground cayenne

½ cup firm tofu, crumbled

½ cup water

2 tablespoons olive oil

2 tablespoons soy sauce

2 teaspoons apple cider vinegar

½ teaspoon liquid smoke

2 sheets frozen vegan puff pastry, thawed

1. Preheat the oven to 350°F. Line a baking sheet with a 9-inch sheet of foil and set aside.

2. In a food processor, combine the vital wheat gluten, tapioca flour, yeast, chili powder, garlic powder, paprika, oregano, cumin, and cayenne. Pulse to mix.

3. In a medium bowl, combine the tofu, water, oil, soy sauce, vinegar, and liquid smoke. Add the wet ingredients to the dry. Process until well mixed.

4. Pinch off a small amount (roughly ¾ tablespoon) of the mixture and shape it into a small log, about ½ inch thick by 1½ inch long. Line up the logs in rows on the foil-covered baking sheet. When you have used up all of the mixture, take another 9-inch sheet of foil and place it on top of the logs. Seal the edges of the foil on all sides.

5. Bake for 15 minutes. Remove from the oven, open the foil packs, and turn the logs. Reseal them in the foil and bake another 10 minutes. Remove from the oven and set aside to cool completely.

6. Roll out the pastry sheets on a lightly floured work surface. Cut the pastry into 2 x 3-inch rectangles. Place a cooled chorizo on the lower third of a pastry rectangle and fold in the sides of the pastry. Roll up the pastry to enclose the chorizo and use your fingers to seal the ends. Place the roll on an ungreased baking sheet, seam side down. Repeat with the remaining ingredients. Refrigerate for 20 minutes or as long as overnight. Preheat the oven to 400°F.

7. Bake until the pastry is nicely browned, about 20 minutes. Serve hot.

make ahead   quick & easy

seitan enchiladas with mole poblano

Baked enchiladas are a great way to use the richly flavored mole poblano sauce. This dish can be prepared ahead of when you need it and then baked when ready to serve. Note: Be sure to make the mole sauce first, as it needs a while to simmer.

Mole Poblano (recipe follows)

2 tablespoons neutral vegetable oil

1 medium yellow onion, finely chopped

1 pound seitan, shredded

½ teaspoon salt

¼ teaspoon freshly ground black pepper

3 garlic cloves, minced

1 tablespoon chili powder

2 teaspoons light brown sugar

⅓ cup coarsely chopped fresh cilantro

½ cup vegetable broth

10 (7-inch) corn tortillas

1. Preheat the oven to 375°F. Lightly grease a 9 x 13-inch baking pan. Spoon a thin layer of the mole poblano sauce on the bottom of the baking pan and set aside.

2. In a large skillet, heat the oil over medium heat. Add the onion, seitan, salt, and pepper, and cook until the onion is softened and the seitan is browned, stirring occasionally, 8 to 10 minutes. Stir in the garlic, chili powder, sugar, and cilantro. Cook for 1 minute. Add the broth and simmer for 3 minutes, then remove from the heat and set aside to cool.

3. Spoon about ⅓ cup of the seitan mixture down the center of 1 tortilla. Roll up and place, seam side down, in the prepared baking pan. Repeat with the remaining tortillas and seitan mixture. Pour the mole sauce over the enchiladas. Cover and bake until hot and bubbly, about 25 minutes. Serve hot. If not using right away, the enchiladas can be assembled ahead of time and then covered and refrigerated for up to 2 days. Bring to room temperature before baking. They can also be tightly wrapped and frozen for up to 2 weeks, then thawed and brought to room temperature before baking.

mole poblano

Mole (pronounced "*mo*-lay") poblano is a rich sauce with multiple flavor layers including ancho chiles, cocoa, and spices. It's an ideal sauce for the enchiladas.

3 dried ancho chiles, seeded

3 tablespoons raisins

1 tablespoon neutral vegetable oil

1 small yellow onion, coarsely chopped

2 garlic cloves, minced

1 (14.5 ounce) can crushed tomatoes

½ cup tortilla chips, crushed

2 tablespoons unsweetened cocoa powder

1 tablespoon white vinegar

1 teaspoon chili powder

1 teaspoon ground coriander

½ teaspoon ground cinnamon

1 cup vegetable broth or water

Salt and freshly ground black pepper

1. In a small heatproof bowl, cover the anchos and the raisins with enough boiling water to cover and soak until softened, about 1 hour. Reserve the soaking liquid.

2. In a medium skillet, heat the oil over medium heat. Add the onion and garlic, cover, and cook until softened, about 5 minutes.

3. In a blender or food processor, puree the soaked anchos and raisins and 1 cup of the soaking liquid in a blender. Add the onion mixture, tomatoes, tortilla chips, cocoa, vinegar, chili powder, coriander, and cinnamon, and process until well blended. The mixture should be thick.

4. Transfer the pureed mixture to a medium saucepan and add the broth and salt and pepper, to taste. Cook, uncovered, over low heat, stirring occasionally, until the sauce is thick but pourable, about 30 minutes. If the sauce is too thick, add a little more broth. Taste and adjust the seasonings, if necessary.

193

make ahead   quick & easy

romaine and avocado salad with cilantro-cumin vinaigrette

MAKES 4 SERVINGS

This crunchy and refreshing salad is an ideal complement to the rest of the meal. To avoid last-minute fussing, make your dressing ahead of time and prepare all the vegetables except the avocados. Then, when you're ready to serve, just add the avocados and dressing and toss.

2 garlic cloves, crushed

½ teaspoon salt

¼ cup minced fresh cilantro

⅓ cup olive oil

3 tablespoons fresh lime juice

1 teaspoon ground cumin

½ teaspoon sugar

¼ teaspoon freshly ground black pepper

1 head romaine lettuce, coarsely chopped

2 ripe Hass avocados, peeled, pitted, and cut into ½-inch dice

⅓ cup pitted and halved kalamata olives

¼ cup coarsely chopped red onion

½ cup halved cherry tomatoes

1. In a blender or food processor, mince the garlic with the salt. Add the cilantro, oil, lime juice, cumin, sugar, and pepper and process until well blended. Taste and adjust seasonings, if necessary. Set aside.

2. In a large bowl, combine the lettuce, avocados, olives, onion, and tomatoes. Pour on the dressing and toss to coat. Serve immediately.

make ahead   **quick & easy**

tres leches cupcakes

MAKES 1 DOZEN CUPCAKES

These tasty cupcakes are inspired by the classic Mexican "three milks" cake. This version uses soy, almond, and coconut milk. The frosting recipe makes a lot, but you can refrigerate or freeze any leftovers.

▪ CUPCAKES

½ cup plain or vanilla soy milk or other nondairy milk

1½ teaspoons apple cider vinegar

¾ cup sugar

¼ cup neutral vegetable oil

¼ cup almond milk

2 tablespoons cream of coconut (the thick top layer of a can of coconut milk)

1½ teaspoons pure vanilla extract

1¼ cups all-purpose flour

½ teaspoon ground cinnamon

1 teaspoon baking powder

¼ teaspoon baking soda

¼ teaspoon salt

▪ FROSTING

⅓ cup vegan margarine

3 cups confectioners' sugar

2 tablespoons plain or vanilla soy milk or other nondairy milk

1 teaspoon pure vanilla extract

½ teaspoon ground cinnamon

1. Make the cupcakes: Preheat the oven to 350°F. Lightly grease a 12-cup muffin tin or line with paper liners and set aside.

2. In a small bowl, combine the soy milk and vinegar and set aside. In a large bowl, combine the sugar, oil, almond milk, cream of coconut, and vanilla, stirring to blend. Stir in the soy milk mixture and set aside.

3. In a medium bowl, combine the flour, cinnamon, baking powder, baking soda, and salt. Mix well. Add the dry ingredients to the wet ingredients and mix until smooth.

4. Pour the batter evenly into the prepared tin about two-thirds full. Bake until a toothpick inserted in the center of a cupcake comes out clean, about 20 minutes. Cool completely on a wire rack before frosting.

5. Make the frosting: In a large bowl, cream the margarine with an electric mixer on high speed until light and fluffy. Add the sugar, soy milk, vanilla, and cinnamon and mix until thoroughly combined. Continue mixing until the frosting is smooth and stiff, about 1 minute. Frost the cooled cupcakes. Serve at once or store in a tightly sealed container at room temperature. These cupcakes taste best if eaten on the same day that they are made.

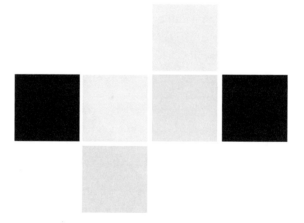

make ahead   quick & easy

mother's day brunch

Nothing pleases a mother more than to have a special meal prepared in her honor. I like the idea of serving a brunch on Mother's Day because it lends itself to being both intimate and elegant and lets your mom feel pampered. Be sure to use your best tableware and an arrangement of fresh flowers and remember to say "Thanks, Mom!"

Preparing a Mother's Day brunch is more personal than taking her to a crowded restaurant, and, unless you live in a city with a vegan restaurant, the chances of finding one that serves a vegan brunch are slim to none.

Of course, Mom shouldn't have all the fun—this brunch menu is also a great way to dazzle weekend guests on a Sunday morning. In fact, a brunch is an easy and economical way to entertain special guests of all kinds, and it makes a nice change from a dinner party. Instead of a formal sit-down brunch for just a few people, you can also serve a more casual-style brunch for a crowd. Check out page 205 for some additional brunch ideas.

the menu

THANKS, MOM! MOTHER'S DAY BRUNCH
Strawberry Carpaccio with Balsamic Syrup
Asparagus Quiche-Me-Not
Tempeh Bacon Triangles
Chai-Spiced Muffins
Chocolate "Pots de Crème"

Go-Withs: *mimosas or bloody Marys, favorite fruit juice, freshly brewed coffee or tea*

recipe swaps

Replace the Strawberry Carpaccio with a soup such as Pea Green Soup (page 163) or a salad such as Baby Greens with Lemony Vinaigrette (page 250).

In place of the quiche, serve Quinoa-Stuffed Portobello Mushrooms with Wine-Braised Shallots (page 251).

Side Dish: Potato Latkes with Cranberry-Apple Relish (page 252).

Dessert: Fresh Berry Tartlets (page 97) or Mixed Berry Crumble (page 220). Alternatively, you can serve vegan vanilla ice cream with a drizzle of chocolate sauce and a tumble of fresh sliced strawberries.

strawberry carpaccio with balsamic syrup

MAKES 4 SERVINGS

Happily, fresh strawberries are just coming into season around Mother's Day, and they can be used in a variety of ways, from appetizers (like this one) to salads or desserts. The balsamic syrup gives the berries a sophisticated flavor and the plate appeal is off-the-charts gorgeous.

½ cup balsamic vinegar

1 tablespoon sugar

1 pint ripe strawberries, hulled

4 mint sprigs, for garnish

1. In a small saucepan, combine the vinegar and sugar and bring to a boil over high heat. Reduce the heat to low and simmer until the syrup reduces, about 10 minutes. Set aside to cool.

2. Set aside 4 whole strawberries for garnish, then cut the remaining strawberries lengthwise into very thin slices (about ⅛ inch thick). Arrange the sliced strawberries on 4 plates, fanned out aesthetically. Drizzle with the balsamic syrup.

3. Cut the remaining 4 strawberries in half lengthwise and arrange 2 halves on each plate as a garnish, nestled with a sprig of mint. Serve immediately.

make ahead   **quick & easy**

asparagus quiche-me-not

Show Mom you love her by serving a delicious quiche made without high-cholesterol eggs and cream. She's guaranteed to love you back.

FILLING

1 pound asparagus, tough ends trimmed

2 tablespoons olive oil

¾ cup minced yellow onion

¾ cup unsalted cashews

¾ cup cooked or canned white beans, drained and rinsed

¼ cup plain unsweetened soy milk or other nondairy milk

2 tablespoons cornstarch

2 tablespoons nutritional yeast

2 teaspoons Dijon mustard

1 teaspoon salt

⅛ teaspoon ground nutmeg

⅛ teaspoon ground cayenne

⅛ teaspoon freshly ground black pepper

2 tablespoons pine nuts

CRUST

1½ cups all-purpose flour

⅓ cup vegan margarine

1 teaspoon sugar

½ teaspoon salt

¼ cup cold water

1. Make the filling: Preheat the oven to 425°F. Place the asparagus spears on a lightly greased baking sheet. Drizzle with 1 tablespoon of the oil. Roast the asparagus until just tender, about 8 minutes. Set aside to cool.

2. In a small skillet, heat the remaining 1 tablespoon oil over medium heat. Add the onion, cover, and cook until soft, about 5 minutes. Remove from the heat.

3. In a food processor or high-speed blender, process the cashews until finely ground. Add the beans and cooked onion and process until smooth. Add the soy milk, cornstarch, yeast, mustard, salt, nutmeg, cayenne, and pepper, and process until well blended. Set aside 6 of the asparagus spears and coarsely chop the remaining asparagus. Add the chopped asparagus

200

to the food processor and pulse to combine. Transfer the mixture to a large bowl and refrigerate while you make the crust.

4. Make the crust: In a food processor, combine the flour, margarine, sugar, and salt and pulse until crumbly. With the machine running, add the water and process to form a dough ball. Remove the dough from the processor, flatten, wrap it in plastic wrap, and refrigerate for 30 minutes.

5. Preheat the oven to 350°F. Roll the dough out into a circle on a lightly floured work surface. Arrange the dough in a fluted quiche pan or pie plate, pressing evenly with your fingers to fit it into the pan, trimming and fluting the edges. Prick the bottom of the crust with the tines of a fork. Cover the edges of the crust with foil to protect from burning and bake the crust for 15 minutes.

6. Remove the crust from the oven and discard the foil. Spoon the filling mixture into the crust and smooth the top. Arrange the reserved asparagus spears on top of the filling in a spoke pattern. Sprinkle with the pine nuts and bake until firm and lightly browned, about 45 minutes. Allow the quiche to cool 15 minutes before cutting. If not using right away, cool to room temperature, then cover and refrigerate for up to 24 hours. When ready to serve, bring to room temperature and warm in the oven, if desired.

make ahead   quick & easy

tempeh bacon triangles

MAKES 8 SERVINGS

Smoky and delicious tempeh bacon makes a nice side dish for any brunch. It's also great in sandwiches and salads. You can also cut the tempeh in any way you like—make strips instead of triangles, or use a cookie cutter to shape the tempeh slices into hearts. The tempeh can be marinated up to 2 days ahead and refrigerated, then quickly browned when ready to serve.

8 ounces tempeh

3 tablespoons soy sauce

1½ teaspoons pure maple syrup

1 teaspoon liquid smoke

2 tablespoons neutral vegetable oil

1. Cut the tempeh in half and then cut each half crosswise to make 4 thin slices. Cut each slice diagonally to make 8 triangles. In a medium saucepan of simmering water, cook the tempeh over medium heat for 20 minutes. Drain and transfer to a shallow baking pan.

2. In a small bowl, combine the soy sauce, maple syrup, and liquid smoke. Pour the mixture on top of the tempeh and marinate for 30 minutes or up to 2 days.

3. In a large skillet, heat the oil over medium heat. Add the tempeh triangles, reserving the marinade, and cook until browned on both sides, about 2 minutes per side. Drizzle with the reserved marinade and cook for 2 more minutes, turning the tempeh to coat. Serve hot.

make ahead   **quick & easy**

chai-spiced muffins

These fragrant muffins taste as good as they smell and are a treat anytime. For an afternoon pick-me-up, enjoy them with a cup of hot coffee or tea, or even some chai.

2 cups all-purpose flour

¼ cup sugar

2 teaspoons baking powder

1 teaspoon baking soda

¾ teaspoon ground cinnamon

½ teaspoon ground coriander

½ teaspoon ground ginger

½ teaspoon ground allspice

¼ teaspoon ground cloves

¼ teaspoon salt

⅛ teaspoon ground black pepper

½ cup vegan vanilla yogurt

½ cup plain or vanilla soy milk

¼ cup pure maple syrup

3 tablespoons neutral vegetable oil

1½ teaspoons pure vanilla extract

1. Preheat the oven to 400°F. Lightly oil a 12-cup muffin tin or line with paper liners and set aside.

2. In a large bowl, combine the flour, sugar, baking powder, baking soda, cinnamon, coriander, ginger, allspice, cloves, salt, and pepper.

3. In a medium bowl, combine the yogurt, soy milk, maple syrup, oil, and vanilla, stirring to blend. Add the wet ingredients to the dry ingredients, stirring to incorporate well. Do not overmix.

4. Spoon the batter into the prepared muffin tin (the batter will be thick). Bake until golden brown and a toothpick inserted into the center of a muffin comes out clean, about 20 minutes. Let cool for 10 minutes on a wire rack. Serve warm. If not using right away, cool the muffins and store at room temperature in an airtight container for up to 12 hours. These muffins taste best if eaten on the same day they are made.

chocolate "pots de crème"

Traditional pot de crème (pronounced *poh duh* KREHM) is a rich cooked pudding prepared and served in small pot-shaped cups. Though this recipe is decidedly nontraditional, it still looks lovely served in pot de crème cups, if you happen to have a set. If not, use tea or coffee cups (as opposed to mugs) or even espresso cups (though the portion will be smaller), and place them on their saucers to make a charming presentation.

1½ cups vegan semisweet chocolate chips

¾ cup slivered raw almonds or unsalted raw cashews

½ cup almond milk or plain or vanilla soy milk

¼ cup agave nectar

¼ cup pure maple syrup

6 ounces firm silken tofu, drained and patted dry

1½ teaspoons pure vanilla extract

Vegan chocolate curls, vegan whipped cream, or coarsely chopped toasted almonds, for garnish (optional)

1. Melt the chocolate chips in a double boiler or microwave. Set aside.

2. In a high-speed blender, grind the almonds to a powder. Add the almond milk and blend until smooth. Add the agave nectar, maple syrup, tofu, and vanilla and blend until smooth. Add the melted chocolate chips and blend until creamy.

3. Pour the filling into serving cups and refrigerate to firm up, at least 2 hours or up to 12 hours. When ready to serve, garnish with your choice of toppings. These are best if eaten on the same day they are made, but should be prepared several hours ahead of time as they need to be refrigerated before serving.

make ahead   **quick & easy**

a brunch-tastic idea

When you're considering having some people over for a casual get-together, think brunch. If you need convincing about the reasons why hosting a brunch may be right for you, here are just some of the advantages:

- Good timing: brunches are traditionally held around noon on a Sunday. This is a convenient time for most people.
- Something different: because it's held at a different time than most parties (and with different food and drink), a brunch makes a nice change from other gatherings, giving it a unique quality.
- Less work for you: a big payoff is that brunches tend to be lower maintenance for the host than a dinner party or other evening get-togethers. Plus, if you work during the week, it gives you all day Saturday to get ready.
- Less expensive: another plus is that brunch food can be less costly than dinner. Also, the amount of alcohol you need is minimal: people don't tend to drink as much at that hour anyway, and the alcoholic beverage can be limited to bloody Marys, mimosas, or Bellinis. Many people will just opt for coffee, tea, and juice.

A brunch can be casual or elegant with a menu such as the Mother's Day Brunch on page 198, or you can simply put on some coffee, chill some juice, cut up some fruit, and make pancakes or waffles to order when your guests arrive.

father's day cookout

This easy and hearty menu makes the most of summer's bounty and is sure to please even an omnivorous father on his special day. For a starter, let Dad munch on some vegetable dippers with creamy ranch-style dressing. Then let him dig into the main event: yummy barbecued "ribz" slathered with a smoky and spicy sauce served with roasted corn, potatoes, and vegetable skewers. Make sure he saves room for dessert because he won't want to miss the luscious Blueberry-Peach Cobbler.

Not just for dads, this menu is great any time you feel like a cookout. The various components are timed so that the grill doesn't need to be crowded all at once. In case of a rainy day, indoor cooking options are provided in the recipes so you can still celebrate Father's Day in style.

the menu

BOYS AND GRILLS

Spicy-Smoky BBQ Ribz
Vegetable Dippers with Ranch Dressing
Foil-Roasted Corn and Potatoes
Grilled Vegetable Skewers
Blueberry-Peach Cobbler

Go-Withs: *vegan vanilla ice cream is great with the cobbler—
even better if you warm the cobbler slightly before serving;
cold beer; grilled garlic bread*

recipe swaps

Appetizer: Chorizo en Croûte (page 190)

Main Dish: Southern Fried Seitan (page 74)

Side Dishes: Fingerling Potato Salad with Pan-Fried
  Arugula Pesto (page 75) and Chilled and Dilled Green
  Beans (page 76)

Dessert: Chocolate Lover's Brownies (page 92)

spicy-smoky bbq ribz

MAKES 4 SERVINGS

Slathered in a rich barbecue sauce, these chewy "ribz" are sure to please any dad on his day. If you want to finish cooking the ribz on the grill, only cook them in the oven for 30 minutes, then you can finish them on the grill—just be careful not to burn them. Cutting the ribz into strips and then arranging them snugly in a pan allows them to pull apart easily after cooking.

BARBECUE SAUCE

1 tablespoon olive oil

½ cup coarsely chopped yellow onion

2 garlic cloves, minced

1 chipotle chile in adobo

½ cup tomato paste

3 tablespoons light brown sugar

2 teaspoons soy sauce

½ teaspoon smoked paprika

½ teaspoon ground cumin

¼ teaspoon dry mustard

3 tablespoons apple cider vinegar

½ cup water

RIBZ

1 chipotle chile in adobo

2 tablespoons olive oil

1 tablespoon soy sauce

1 teaspoon liquid smoke

1 tablespoon nutritional yeast

1½ teaspoons smoked paprika

½ teaspoon garlic powder

½ teaspoon onion powder

½ teaspoon salt

1 cup vital wheat gluten (wheat gluten flour)

¾ cup water

1. Make the barbecue sauce: In a medium saucepan, heat the oil over medium heat. Add the onion, cover, and cook until softened, about 5 minutes. Add the garlic, chipotle, tomato paste, sugar, soy sauce, paprika, cumin, and mustard. Stir in the vinegar and water and bring to a boil. Reduce the heat to low, cover, and simmer for 30 minutes.

2. Make the ribz: Preheat the oven to 350°F. Lightly grease an 8-inch square baking pan and set aside.

3. In a food processor, puree the chipotle with the oil, soy sauce, liquid smoke, and 1 tablespoon of the barbecue sauce. Add the yeast, paprika, garlic powder, onion powder, and salt and process to blend. Add the vital wheat gluten and water and process until well mixed.

4. Turn the seitan mixture out onto a flat work surface and use your hands to flatten it into an 8-inch square. Cut the seitan into quarters and cut each quarter into three slices. Arrange the seitan slices in the prepared pan (it's okay if they touch and fit snuggly). Cover tightly with foil and bake for 30 minutes.

5. Remove the seitan from the oven and spread about ⅓ cup of the barbecue sauce on top. Use a metal spatula to turn the seitan over. Brush the top with another ⅓ cup of the barbecue sauce. Cover with foil and return to the oven for 15 minutes. Remove from the oven, spread more barbecue sauce over the seitan, and bake uncovered for 10 minutes more. Transfer the seitan to a work surface and recut into "ribz" before serving. Serve immediately.

M make ahead   ⓠ quick & easy

father'sdaycookout

vegetable dippers with ranch dressing

Vary the veggies according to your own taste and preference. If you're using the dressing on the same day it's made, you can use fresh parsley and chives (and add other fresh herbs, if desired). However, if you're making the dressing a day or two ahead of time, it's best to use all dried herbs.

½ cup vegan mayonnaise

¼ cup vegan sour cream

¼ cup plain unsweetened soy milk or other nondairy milk

1 tablespoon apple cider vinegar

2 tablespoons minced fresh parsley

1 teaspoon minced fresh chives (optional)

½ teaspoon dried dill weed

¼ teaspoon onion powder

¼ teaspoon garlic powder

⅛ teaspoon ground cayenne

⅛ teaspoon freshly ground black pepper

⅛ teaspoon salt

2 cups small broccoli or cauliflower florets, lightly steamed

4 ounces green beans, trimmed and lightly steamed

2 carrots, cut into 4-inch sticks, about ¼ inch thick

2 celery ribs, cut into 4-inch sticks, about ¼ inch thick

1 yellow or red bell pepper, cut lengthwise into ¼-inch strips

1 thin cucumber, peeled and cut lengthwise into spears

5 radishes, trimmed

5 cherry or grape tomatoes

1. In a food processor or blender, combine the mayonnaise, sour cream, soy milk, vinegar, parsley, chives (if using), dill weed, onion powder, garlic powder, cayenne, black pepper, and salt. Blend until smooth. Transfer to a small bowl.

2. Place the bowl of dressing in the center of a round platter and arrange the vegetables (except for the radishes and tomatoes) aesthetically around it, keeping each type of vegetable separate. Place the radishes and tomatoes individually among the vegetables to add color interest. Serve immediately. If not using right away, cover and refrigerate the dressing for up to 2 days (see headnote). The vegetables may be tightly wrapped and refrigerated for several hours but are best if used on the same day they are prepared.

foil-roasted corn and potatoes

MAKES 4 SERVINGS

These summertime favorites are great on the grill and so easy to make when wrapped in foil. The optional addition of fresh herbs to the corn adds wonderful and unexpected flavor notes.

4 medium russet or Yukon
  gold potatoes, unpeeled and
  scrubbed
Olive oil

Salt
8 ears corn, husks left on
Fresh basil, thyme, or other
  herbs (optional)

1. Preheat the grill. Rub each potato with a small amount of oil and season with salt. Wrap each potato in a sheet of foil and place them on the grill, away from the hottest part of the grill. Close the lid and allow the potatoes to roast until softened, turning occasionally, 45 minutes to 1 hour, depending on the size of the potatoes.

2. Remove the tough outer husks on the corn, leaving the inner husks. Carefully pull back the inner husks; do not remove. Remove all the corn silk and discard. Rub the corn kernels with a small amount of oil and a few sprigs of fresh herbs, if using. Bring the inner husks back up around the corn and wrap each ear in foil. Place the corn on the hot grill and cook, turning frequently to cook evenly and prevent charring, 8 to 10 minutes. Pile the corn and potatoes on a platter and serve immediately.

Variation: Bake the potatoes in a 425°F oven until soft, about 1 hour. Cook the corn in a large pot of unsalted boiling water for 2 to 3 minutes.

211

make ahead   quick & easy

grilled vegetable skewers

Some say everything tastes better cooked on a grill and these colorful and delicious skewered vegetables are no exception. I like this particular combination of vegetables, but you can change it up according to your own preference. The skewers can be assembled several hours ahead of time and refrigerated, then brought to room temperature when ready to grill.

1 medium red onion, quartered and separated

1 medium yellow bell pepper, cut into 1½-inch squares

2 small zucchini, cut into 1-inch chunks

2 small yellow summer squash, cut into 1-inch chunks

12 white mushrooms, lightly rinsed and patted dry

12 cherry tomatoes

2 tablespoons olive oil

1 tablespoon soy sauce

Salt and freshly ground black pepper

1. Soak bamboo skews in water for 30 minutes. Preheat the grill. Lightly steam the onion, bell pepper, zucchini, and summer squash for 2 minutes to soften slightly. Set aside to cool. Steam the mushrooms for 1 minute and set aside to cool.

2. Thread the steamed vegetables and the cherry tomatoes alternately on the soaked skewers. Drizzle with oil and soy sauce and season with salt and black pepper, to taste.

3. Place the vegetable skewers on the hot grill and cook until slightly charred, turning once, about 4 minutes per side. Serve immediately.

Variation: To cook indoors, preheat the oven to 425°F. Place the seasoned vegetable skewers on an ungreased baking sheet and roast until nicely browned, about 10 minutes.

blueberry-peach cobbler

Show Dad you care with a delicious homey dessert made with the fresh fruit of the season. Blueberries and peaches make a wonderful combination, both visually and flavor-wise. For an added treat, serve with a scoop of vegan vanilla ice cream.

4 ripe peaches, peeled, pitted, and cut into ¼-inch slices
1½ cups fresh blueberries
¾ cup sugar
1 tablespoon cornstarch
½ teaspoon ground cinnamon
¼ teaspoon ground ginger

1½ cups all-purpose flour
2 teaspoons baking powder
½ teaspoon salt
⅓ cup vegan margarine, melted
½ cup plain or vanilla soy milk or other nondairy milk

1. Preheat the oven to 375°F. In a large bowl, combine the peaches, blueberries, ½ cup of the sugar, cornstarch, cinnamon, and ginger, stirring gently to mix.

2. Spoon the fruit mixture into the bottom of an ungreased 9-inch square baking pan and set aside.

3. In a separate large bowl, combine the flour, baking powder, salt, and remaining ¼ cup sugar. Blend in the margarine and the soy milk until a soft dough forms. Drop the dough by large spoonfuls on top of the fruit mixture. Bake until the fruit is bubbly and the crust is golden brown, about 45 minutes. Serve warm. The cobbler can be made several hours ahead of time and kept at room temperature until serving time, rewarming for a few minutes in the oven, if desired.

make ahead   **quick & easy**

a fourth of july celebration

I love it when holiday colors can play into the theme of the food I'm preparing. So naturally, when I plan a gathering on the Fourth of July, you'll see lots of red, white, and blue on the dinner table. This menu can be enjoyed both indoors and out, which can be handy when the weather doesn't cooperate. And of course, Independence Day isn't the only time you'll want to enjoy this all-American menu. The corn cakes are great not only as an appetizer, but also as a side dish. The burgers and both salads are ideal for easy weeknight meals and the berry crumble makes a tasty dessert anytime.

the menu

STARS AND STRIPES FOREVER

Mini Blue Corn Pancakes with
  Chipotle-Streaked Sour Cream
Independence Burgers
Three-Potato Salad
Herbed Vegetable Salad
Mixed Berry Crumble

Go-Withs: pickles; red, white, and blue vegetable chips;
cold beverages of choice

recipe swaps

Appetizer: Vegetable Dippers with Ranch Dressing
  (page 210)

Salads: Super Slaw (page 146); Shamrock Vegetable
  Salad (page 165); or Fingerling Potato Salad with
  Pan-Fried Arugula Pesto (page 75)

Main Dish: Seitan Buffalo Wingz (page 112);
  Southern Fried Seitan (page 74); or Spicy-Smoky BBQ
  Ribz (page 208)

Dessert: Blueberry-Peach Cobbler (page 213) or
  Caramel Almond-Oat Bars (page 77)

mini blue corn pancakes with chipotle-streaked sour cream

MAKES 6 SERVINGS

These tasty corn cakes made with blue cornmeal are paired with a smoky sour cream for an appetizer that's all decked out in red, white, and blue. If you can't find blue cornmeal, the regular yellow kind is fine and tastes the same.

½ cup vegan sour cream
1 chipotle chile in adobo, minced
½ cup blue cornmeal
½ cup all-purpose flour
1 teaspoon baking powder
¼ teaspoon salt

⅛ teaspoon sugar
½ cup plain unsweetened soy milk or other nondairy milk
1½ cups fresh or thawed frozen corn kernels
Neutral vegetable oil, for frying

1. Place the sour cream in a small bowl. Add the chipotle and use a fork to "drag" it decoratively through the top of the sour cream. Set aside. Preheat the oven to 250°F.

2. In a large bowl, combine the cornmeal, flour, baking powder, salt, and sugar and mix well. Stir in the soy milk, then add the corn and stir to combine.

3. In a large skillet, heat a thin layer of oil over medium heat. Drop the batter by the heaping teaspoonful into the skillet, and fry until golden brown, turning once, about 2 minutes per side. Transfer cooked pancakes to a heatproof platter and keep warm in the oven while you cook the rest. Serve immediately with the sour cream. If not using right away, cool the pancakes to room temperature, then cover and refrigerate for up to 3 days. They can be warmed in the oven for a few minutes when ready to serve.

independence burgers

MAKES 4 BURGERS

With these great-tasting and meaty-looking burgers, you can gain your independence from store-bought veggie burgers. They freeze well, so you can make them in advance to avoid last-minute fussing.

1 cup cooked or canned black beans, drained and rinsed

½ cup walnut pieces

¼ cup coarsely chopped yellow onion

½ cup vital wheat gluten (wheat gluten flour)

2 tablespoons soy sauce

½ teaspoon browning sauce

½ teaspoon onion powder

¼ teaspoon salt

⅛ teaspoon freshly ground black pepper

Olive oil, for frying

4 burger rolls, lightly toasted

1. In a food processor, process the beans, walnuts, and onion until finely chopped. Add the vital wheat gluten, soy sauce, browning sauce, onion powder, salt, and pepper. Process until well combined, but with some texture remaining.

2. Shape the mixture into 4 patties, adding a little more flour if the mixture is too wet. Place the burgers on a plate and refrigerate for 20 minutes or overnight (if making well in advance, tightly wrap the burgers and freeze for up to 1 month).

3. In a large skillet, heat a thin layer of oil over medium heat. Add the burgers and cook until browned on both sides, turning once, about 4 minutes per side. Serve on the rolls with your favorite condiments.

make ahead   **quick & easy**

three-potato salad

Made with a combination of red, white, and blue potatoes, this is one patriotic potato salad—and it tastes great too. Best of all, it's equally yummy if you only use one type of potato, so there's no need to reserve it for Independence Day alone.

8 ounces Peruvian Blue potatoes, unpeeled and scrubbed

8 ounces small red-skinned potatoes, unpeeled and scrubbed

8 ounces small white potatoes, unpeeled

1/3 cup minced celery

1/4 cup minced green onions

2 tablespoons minced fresh parsley

1/3 cup olive oil

2 tablespoons apple cider vinegar

1/2 teaspoon salt

1/8 teaspoon freshly ground black pepper

1/8 teaspoon sugar

1. Halve or quarter the potatoes so that they are a uniform size. In a large pot of boiling salted water, cook the potatoes until tender but still firm, about 15 minutes. Drain well and transfer to a large bowl. Add the celery, green onions, and parsley. Set aside.

2. In a small bowl, combine the oil, vinegar, salt, pepper, and sugar. Pour the dressing over the potato mixture and toss gently to combine. Taste and adjust seasonings, if necessary.

make ahead   **quick & easy**

herbed vegetable salad

Although it's a departure from the red, white, and blue theme, I like to include this refreshing vegetable salad on my Fourth of July menu. After all, we shouldn't skip our vegetables just because it's a holiday.

1 medium fennel bulb, coarsely chopped

1 medium red bell pepper, coarsely chopped

1 large carrot, coarsely chopped

1 medium cucumber, peeled, seeded, and coarsely chopped

1 cup cherry or grape tomatoes, halved

¼ cup minced red onion

1 cup cooked or 1 (15.5-ounce) can chickpeas, drained and rinsed

¼ cup chopped pitted kalamata olives

1 garlic clove, minced

2 tablespoons fresh lemon juice

¼ teaspoon salt

Freshly ground black pepper

Pinch sugar

¼ cup olive oil

3 tablespoons coarsely chopped, fresh parsley

3 tablespoons coarsely chopped fresh basil

1. In a large bowl, combine the fennel, bell pepper, carrot, cucumber, tomatoes, onion, chickpeas, and olives. Set aside.

2. In a small bowl, combine the garlic, juice, salt, black pepper, to taste, and sugar. Add the oil, stirring to blend.

3. Sprinkle the parsley and basil over the vegetables. Add the dressing and toss gently to combine. Serve at room temperature. If not using right away, cover and refrigerate until needed. This salad can be made several hours in advance but tastes best if eaten on the same day that it is made.

mixed berry crumble

In many parts of the United States, watermelon is the official dessert of Independence Day get-togethers. But I also like to include a dessert that features the fresh red and blue berries of the season. You can make this crumble several hours in advance and then warm it for a few minutes in the oven when ready to serve.

2 cups strawberries, hulled and cut into ¼-inch slices
2 cups blueberries
1 cup raspberries or blackberries
½ cup granulated sugar
1½ tablespoons cornstarch
½ teaspoon ground cinnamon

¼ teaspoon ground ginger
¾ cup all-purpose flour
⅔ cup light brown sugar
¼ cup old-fashioned oats or finely chopped pecans
½ cup vegan margarine, cut into small pieces

1. Preheat the oven to 375°F. Place the berries in a 9-inch square baking pan and sprinkle with the granulated sugar, cornstarch, ¼ teaspoon of the cinnamon, and the ginger. Stir to mix well and set aside.

2. In a medium bowl, combine the flour, brown sugar, oats, and remaining ¼ teaspoon cinnamon. Mix well. Use a pastry blender or fork to cut in the margarine until the mixture resembles coarse crumbs.

3. Spread the topping over the berries and bake until the topping is browned and the berry mixture is bubbling, about 30 minutes. Serve warm.

make ahead   quick & easy

halloween

Halloween party food should be fun and thematic to mirror the occasion. Accordingly, every item on this menu is orange and black, which can make quite an impact on a buffet table. While these dishes are "spook-tacular" together, each dish can be enjoyed individually for any occasion.

I've designed this menu as a buffet, since on Halloween you're more likely to have a casual get-together on Halloween where guests mill around in costume rather than sit around a formal dining table. This is one occasion where it's nearly impossible to overdo the decorations. Consider serving your chili in a large hollowed-out pumpkin and using orange and black tableware.

Because all the dishes in this menu are designed with the orange and black theme in mind, there are no "subs and swaps" offered, although you could certainly pare down the menu somewhat by omitting the tapenade and crudités as well as the rice salad. If you'd like to serve a tossed salad with the chili and muffins, you could serve it in an orange or black bowl and garnish it with shredded carrots and pitted black olives to keep the theme going.

the menu

HALLOWEEN BOO-FFET

*Black Olive Tapenade with Carrot Sticks
  and Orange Bell Pepper Strips*
Black Bean and Butternut Chili
Savory Pumpkin Muffins with Black Sesame Seeds
Black Rice Salad
Orange-Carrot Cake with Dark Chocolate Icing

Go-Withs: *apple cider*

recipe swaps

Since this menu is very color specific—orange
and black—there are no recipe swaps for this
chapter.

black olive tapenade with carrot sticks and orange bell pepper strips

MAKES 6 SERVINGS

Tapenade served with bright orange crudités is a dramatic addition to any Halloween get-together. To heighten the visual effect, serve the tapenade in a hollowed-out orange bell pepper and set it in a black bowl or on a black platter surrounded by the carrots and pepper strips.

1 cup pitted kalamata olives
2 tablespoons capers, rinsed
1 garlic clove, minced
1 tablespoon minced fresh
  parsley
2 teaspoons fresh lemon juice
Freshly ground black pepper

2 tablespoons olive oil
3 large carrots, cut into 4-inch-
  long sticks about ¼ inch thick
2 orange bell peppers, halved
  lengthwise and cut into
  ¼-inch-wide strips

1. In a food processor, combine the olives, capers, garlic, and parsley and pulse until finely chopped. Add the lemon juice and a few grinds of black pepper. Add the oil and process to a paste. Transfer the tapenade to a small bowl.

2. To serve, arrange the carrots and bell peppers decoratively on a platter with the tapenade. The tapenade can be made several days in advance and covered and refrigerated until needed. The vegetables can be cut several hours in advance and covered and refrigerated until serving.

make ahead   **quick & easy**

black bean and butternut chili

Halloween colors play out deliciously in this flavorful chili made with black beans and diced butternut squash. It makes a great centerpiece on a buffet table when served out of a large pumpkin shell. You can also serve it in a Crock-Pot on the "keep warm" setting.

1 small butternut squash, peeled, halved, and seeded

1 tablespoon olive oil

1 medium yellow onion, coarsely chopped

1 medium carrot, finely chopped

1 medium orange bell pepper, coarsely chopped (optional)

1 (14.5-ounce) can crushed tomatoes

2 tablespoons tomato paste

4 cups cooked or 3 (15.5-ounce) cans black beans, drained and rinsed

1 chipotle chile in adobo, minced

1 cup apple juice

3 tablespoons chili powder

½ teaspoon ground allspice

½ teaspoon sugar

Salt and freshly ground black pepper

1. Cut the squash into ¼-inch dice and set aside. In a large saucepan, heat the oil over medium heat. Add the onion, squash, carrot, and bell pepper, if using. Cover and cook until softened, about 10 minutes.

2. Add the tomatoes, tomato paste, beans, and chipotle. Stir in the apple juice, chili powder, allspice, sugar, and salt and black pepper, to taste. Bring to a boil, then reduce the heat to low. Simmer, covered, until the vegetables are tender, about 30 minutes, stirring occasionally.

3. Uncover and simmer about 10 minutes longer. Serve immediately. If not using right away, bring to room temperature, then cover and refrigerate for up to 3 days or freeze for up to 2 weeks, then thaw before reheating.

savory pumpkin muffins with black sesame seeds

MAKES 1 DOZEN MUFFINS

Luscious pumpkin muffins dotted with black sesame seeds are all set for Halloween. In addition to being a delicious accompaniment to the chili, these muffins are simply adorable.

1¼ cups all-purpose flour
½ cup yellow cornmeal
2 teaspoons baking powder
½ teaspoon baking soda
½ teaspoon salt
1¼ cups canned solid-pack pumpkin
¼ cup light brown sugar
½ cup plain soy milk or other nondairy milk

½ cup neutral vegetable oil
¼ cup minced canned green chiles (hot or mild)
¼ cup finely chopped unsalted pumpkin seeds
2 tablespoons black sesame seeds

1. Preheat the oven to 375°F. Lightly grease a 12-cup muffin tin or line with paper liners and set aside.

2. In a large bowl, combine the flour, cornmeal, baking powder, baking soda, and salt. Set aside.

3. In a medium bowl, combine the pumpkin, sugar, soy milk, and oil.

4. Mix the wet ingredients into the dry ingredients until just combined. Stir in the green chiles and pumpkin seeds.

5. Transfer the batter to the prepared pan. Sprinkle the tops of the muffins with the black sesame seeds. Bake until a toothpick inserted in the center of a muffin comes out clean, 16 to 18 minutes. Let cool for 5 minutes before removing from the pan. Serve warm or at room temperature. These muffins taste best if eaten on the same day they are made, but can be baked several hours ahead and stored at room temperature until needed.

make ahead   **quick & easy**

halloween

black rice salad

Black rice is a delicious nutty variety of rice that actually appears more deep purple than black. Combined with orange vegetables and a lemony vinaigrette, it makes a "spook-tacular" salad for a Halloween party buffet.

1 large sweet potato, peeled and cut into ½-inch dice
¼ cup plus 1 tablespoon olive oil
Salt and freshly ground black pepper
2 medium carrots, shredded
1 medium orange bell pepper, finely chopped
¼ cup minced yellow onion
2 tablespoons minced fresh parsley

1½ cups cooked or 1 (15.5-ounce) can chickpeas, drained and rinsed
3 cups cold cooked black rice
3 tablespoons fresh lemon juice
1 teaspoon minced garlic
½ teaspoon dry mustard
Shredded romaine lettuce, for serving
Carrot curls, for garnish

1. Preheat the oven to 425°F. Spread the sweet potatoes on a lightly greased baking sheet and drizzle with 1 tablespoon of the oil. Season with salt and black pepper and roast until tender, about 15 minutes. Set aside to cool.

2. In a large bowl, combine the carrots, bell pepper, onion, parsley, and chickpeas. Add the rice and the roasted sweet potatoes and set aside.

3. In a small bowl, combine the lemon juice, garlic, mustard, ½ teaspoon salt, and ¼ teaspoon black pepper. Whisk in the remaining ¼ cup oil, pour the dressing over the salad mixture, and toss to combine. Taste and adjust the seasonings, if necessary. To serve, spoon the salad into a large shallow serving bowl lined with the lettuce and topped with the carrot curls. The rice salad can be made a day in advance and covered and refrigerated until needed. (Hold off on spooning it into a lettuce-lined bowl until ready to serve.)

orange-carrot cake with dark chocolate icing

MAKES 8 SERVINGS

Spread the icing evenly over the cake or pipe from a pastry bag in the shape of a spiderweb with a chocolate spider off to one side.

CAKE

2 cups all-purpose flour

2 teaspoons baking powder

1 teaspoon baking soda

2 teaspoons ground cinnamon

1 teaspoon salt

1 cup light brown sugar

½ cup fresh orange juice

½ cup neutral vegetable oil

¼ cup pure maple syrup

2 teaspoons pure vanilla extract

2¼ cups finely shredded carrots

2 tablespoons minced orange zest

ICING

6 tablespoons vegan margarine, softened

1 teaspoon orange extract

⅔ cup unsweetened cocoa powder

2⅔ cups confectioners' sugar

¼ cup plain or vanilla soy milk or other nondairy milk

2 tablespoons fresh orange juice

1. Make the cake: Preheat the oven to 350°F. Lightly grease a 9-inch square baking pan and set aside. In a large bowl, mix together the flour, baking powder, baking soda, cinnamon, and salt.

2. In a medium bowl, combine the sugar, juice, oil, maple syrup, and vanilla. Add the wet ingredients to the dry ingredients. Stir in the carrots and orange zest until just mixed.

3. Scrape the batter into the prepared pan. Bake until a toothpick comes out clean, 40 to 45 minutes. Let the cake cool in the pan for 15 minutes, then invert onto a wire rack to cool completely.

4. Make the icing: In a large bowl, cream the margarine with the orange extract. Beat in the cocoa and sugar, a little at a time, adding the soy milk and juice between additions. Continue beating until smooth, adding a bit more soy milk if needed. When the cake is completely cool, frost the cake with the icing.

make ahead　　**quick & easy**

simply
stuffed
thanksgiving
dinner

Preparing Thanksgiving dinner can be stressful, especially for new vegans whose extended families may be accustomed to a turkey on the table. Let these guests discover how tasty a turkey-free Thanksgiving can be with this menu of delicious seasonal dishes.

In my experience, I've found that including at least some familiar dishes in the menu, such as stuffing, mashed potatoes, and gravy, helps to quell the anxiety of relatives who may think they'll starve if they can't eat meat. If you have some favorite family side dishes, you might want to include them in your menu to provide a familiar touchstone.

the menu

PILGRIM'S PROGRESS
Chestnut Bisque
Buttercup Squash Stuffed with Wild Rice,
    Shiitakes, and Caramelized Leeks
Pan Gravy
Roasted Autumn Vegetables
Cranberry-Apple Relish
Pecan-Pumpkin Pie

Go-Withs: dinner rolls; wine, coffee, tea

recipe swaps

The menu for Christmas dinner (page 239)
makes a wonderful Thanksgiving dinner as
well. The various dishes can also be mixed and
matched according to your own preferences.

chestnut bisque

This rich velvety soup is a wonderful way to begin a festive meal. Jarred or frozen peeled chestnuts will cut down on your preparation time considerably. If using fresh chestnuts, see the instructions below and plan to prepare them in advance.

2½ cups cooked and peeled chestnuts (see note below)

1 tablespoon plus 1 teaspoon olive oil

½ cup chopped yellow onion

2 celery ribs, coarsely chopped

1 tablespoon chopped fresh parsley

1 teaspoon minced fresh thyme

4 cups vegetable broth

⅛ teaspoon ground nutmeg

Salt and freshly ground black pepper

1 tablespoon brandy (optional)

Finely minced celery leaves, for garnish

1. Thinly slice 4 chestnuts and set aside. In a large saucepan, heat the 1 tablespoon oil over medium heat. Add the onion and celery. Cover and cook until softened, about 8 minutes. Uncover and add the remaining chestnuts, parsley, thyme, broth, nutmeg, and salt and pepper, to taste. Bring to a boil, then reduce the heat to low and simmer, covered, for 30 minutes.

2. Heat the remaining 1 teaspoon oil in a small skillet over medium heat. Add the reserved chestnuts and cook until browned. Remove from the heat and set aside.

3. Puree the soup in a blender and return to the pot. Heat over medium heat until hot and add the brandy, if using. If the soup is too thick, add ½ cup more broth. To serve, ladle the soup into bowls and garnish with celery leaves and the chestnuts. If not using right away, cool to room temperature, then cover and refrigerate for up to 2 days. Reheat when ready to serve.

Note: *If using fresh chestnuts preheat the oven to 400°F. Use a sharp paring knife to cut an X on the flat side of each chestnut shell and arrange on a baking sheet. Roast until the shells begin to curl open, 15 to 20 minutes. While still warm, remove the outer shell and inner skin of each chestnut.*

buttercup squash stuffed with wild rice, shiitakes, and caramelized leeks

MAKES 4 SERVINGS

If a "tofu turkey" isn't high on your list for Thanksgiving main dish ideas, you might prefer this stuffed squash. It makes a lovely presentation and if you can find a squash large enough, you can actually "carve" it at the table. The stuffing recipe makes about four cups—enough to fill one large or two smaller squashes.

½ cup wild rice

2½ cups water

Salt

½ cup long-grain brown rice

1 large buttercup or other winter squash, halved and seeded

2 leeks, trimmed

2 tablespoons neutral vegetable oil

2 teaspoons light brown sugar

½ cup minced yellow onion

¼ cup minced celery

2½ cups chopped shiitake mushrooms

1 teaspoon minced fresh thyme or ½ teaspoon dried

1 teaspoon minced fresh sage or ½ teaspoon dried

¼ teaspoon freshly ground black pepper

¼ cup minced fresh parsley

1. In a medium saucepan, combine the wild rice and water, cover, and bring to a boil over high heat. Reduce the heat to medium-low, salt the water, and cook, covered, for 30 minutes. Stir in the brown rice, cover, and cook 40 minutes longer. When the rice is cooked, remove from the heat and set aside, covered. If any liquid remains, drain it off. Preheat the oven to 350°F. Lightly grease a 9 x 13-inch baking pan and set aside.

2. Season the squash halves with salt and place them in the prepared pan, cut side down. Add ¼ inch of water to the pan and cover tightly with foil. Bake until slightly softened, about 30 minutes.

3. Split the leeks lengthwise, wash thoroughly, and finely slice them. In a medium skillet, heat 1 tablespoon of the oil over medium heat. Add the

231

make ahead   quick & easy

leeks, season with salt, and cook, uncovered, for 10 minutes, stirring occasionally. Sprinkle with the sugar and continue to cook, stirring occasionally, until nicely browned and soft, about 15 minutes. Stir in a tablespoon or two of water if the leeks begin to stick. Remove from the heat and set aside.

4. In a large skillet, heat the remaining 1 tablespoon oil over medium heat. Add the onion and celery and cook until softened, about 7 minutes. Stir in the mushrooms, thyme, sage, pepper, and salt, to taste. Cook until the mushrooms are softened, stirring occasionally, about 5 minutes. Transfer the mushroom mixture to a large bowl. Add the cooked rice, leeks, and parsley and season with salt, to taste. Mix thoroughly to combine well.

5. Turn the baked squash over, cut side up, and fill the squash with the stuffing. Cover with foil and bake until the stuffing is hot and the squash is tender, about 30 minutes. Serve hot. This recipe can be made ahead up to the final 30-minute baking time: prepare the recipe to that point, then cover and refrigerate for up to 1 day, then bring to room temperature before baking.

pan gravy

This richly flavored gravy is wonderful on the stuffed squash. It's also especially good spooned over mashed potatoes or sautéed seitan.

2 tablespoons olive oil

½ cup finely chopped yellow onion

2 garlic cloves, minced

1 teaspoon minced fresh thyme or ½ teaspoon dried

1 teaspoon minced fresh sage or ½ teaspoon dried

¼ cup all-purpose flour

2 cups vegetable broth

2 teaspoons tomato paste

¼ cup dry red wine

2 tablespoons soy sauce

¾ teaspoon browning liquid

1. In a large saucepan, heat the oil over medium heat. Add the onion, cover, and cook, stirring occasionally, until softened and lightly browned, about 10 minutes. Uncover, add the garlic, thyme, and sage, and cook 1 minute longer.

2. Sprinkle the flour over the onion and cook, stirring, until the flour is absorbed. Cook for another minute and add 1 cup of the broth.

3. When the mixture thickens, stir in the remaining 1 cup broth, tomato paste, wine, and soy sauce. Stir until the mixture becomes smooth. Cover and simmer over low heat for 15 minutes. Stir in the browning liquid.

4. Puree the sauce in a blender or food processor and return to the saucepan. Serve hot. If not using right away, cool to room temperature, then refrigerate in a tightly covered container for up to 3 days and reheat when ready to serve.

make ahead   **quick & easy**

roasted autumn vegetables

Roasting brings out the naturally sweet flavor of vegetables complemented by a sprinkling of herbs. Serve with the stuffed squash and Cranberry-Apple Relish and you'll have all the colors of autumn on your plate.

2 cups Brussels sprouts, blanched

2 large carrots, cut into ½-inch slices

2 medium parsnips, peeled and cut into ½-inch slices

2 medium Yukon gold potatoes, peeled and cut into 1-inch chunks

1 large red onion, cut into ½-inch dice

2 tablespoons olive oil

½ teaspoon dried marjoram

½ teaspoon dried sage

½ teaspoon dried thyme

½ teaspoon salt

¼ teaspoon freshly ground black pepper

1 tablespoon minced fresh parsley, for garnish

1. Preheat the oven to 425°F. Lightly grease a 9 x 13-inch baking pan.

2. To the prepared pan, add the Brussels sprouts, carrots, parsnips, potatoes, and onion. Add the oil, marjoram, sage, thyme, salt, and pepper. Toss the vegetables to coat.

3. Spread the vegetables in a single layer and roast, stirring occasionally, until tender and just beginning to brown, about 45 minutes. Serve hot, sprinkled with the parsley.

cranberry-apple relish

Layered with flavor, this sophisticated relish is a nice change from regular cranberry sauce.

1 (12-ounce) package fresh cranberries

1 crisp apple, peeled, cored, and finely chopped

1 cup light brown sugar

½ teaspoon grated fresh ginger

1 teaspoon ground cinnamon

2 tablespoons balsamic vinegar

2 tablespoons pomegranate molasses

2 tablespoons water

1. In a large saucepan, combine all the ingredients and bring to a boil. Reduce the heat to low and simmer, stirring frequently, until the cranberries pop and the apple is tender, about 15 minutes. Remove from the heat and set aside to cool.

2. Transfer to a serving bowl and refrigerate for at least 1 hour before serving. This relish can be made several hours in advance but tastes best if eaten on the same day that it is made.

make ahead　　**quick & easy**

pecan-pumpkin pie

Your favorite pumpkin pie just got better—with a luscious pecan topping that adds a wonderful flavor and texture to this Thanksgiving institution. Since this pie needs to refrigerate for several hours before serving, it's an ideal make-ahead dessert. It can be made up to a day in advance, although I think it tastes best if eaten on the same day that it is made.

CRUST

1¼ cups all-purpose flour

½ teaspoon sugar

¼ teaspoon salt

½ cup vegan margarine, cut into small pieces

3 tablespoons ice water, plus more if needed

TOPPING

1 cup coarsely chopped pecans

⅓ cup pure maple syrup

2 tablespoons vegan margarine, melted

FILLING

1 (16-ounce) can solid-pack pumpkin

4 ounces firm silken tofu, drained and patted dry

3 tablespoons pure maple syrup

1 teaspoon pure vanilla extract

½ cup granulated sugar

½ cup light brown sugar

2 teaspoons ground cinnamon

½ teaspoon ground allspice

½ teaspoon ground ginger

½ teaspoon ground nutmeg

⅛ teaspoon ground cloves

⅛ teaspoon salt

1 tablespoon cornstarch

1 teaspoon baking powder

1. Make the crust: In a food processor, combine the flour, sugar, and salt, pulsing to blend. Add the margarine and pulse to combine until the mixture resembles coarse crumbs. Add the water a little at a time and pulse until the dough just starts to hold together. Remove the dough from the food processor and shape it into a disk. Wrap it in plastic wrap and refrigerate for 30 minutes.

236

2. Make the topping: In a small bowl, combine the pecans, maple syrup, and margarine. Stir to combine. Set aside. Preheat the oven to 350°F.

3. Make the filling: In a food processor, combine the pumpkin, tofu, maple syrup, and vanilla, and process until well blended. Add both sugars, cinnamon, allspice, ginger, nutmeg, cloves, salt, cornstarch, and baking powder. Process until smooth and well combined.

4. Roll out the dough on a lightly floured work surface to about 10 inches in diameter. Fit the dough into a 9-inch pie plate. Trim and flute the edges. Pour the filling into the crust. Bake for 30 minutes.

5. Remove from the oven and sprinkle with the pecan topping. Return to the oven and bake 30 minutes longer. Let cool to room temperature on a wire rack, then chill in the refrigerator for 5 hours or until set.

make ahead   quick & easy

christmas

Christmas dinner ranks up there with Thanksgiving in terms of family food traditions, though many of them are not traditionally vegan. So, in order to keep everyone at the table happy, from vegans to omnivores, I've developed a menu that includes many traditional flavors but which is still vegan.

This menu begins with a salad, but a soup (such as the Chestnut Bisque, page 230) can be served instead. It also features a seitan roast as the main dish, along with a flavorful mushroom sauce and mashed potatoes. For a festive side, we have wilted spinach with dried cranberries and Spiced Two-Apple Tart for dessert. This easy and elegant menu doesn't need to wait for Christmas—try it any time you want to make your family or guests feel special.

the menu

CHRISTMAS DINNER

Mixed Greens with Caramelized Walnuts
  and Balsamic Pear Vinaigrette
Porcini-Stuffed Seitan with Wild Mushroom Sauce
Herb-Mashed Potatoes
Wilted Baby Spinach with Dried Cranberries
Spiced Two-Apple Tart with Cider Crème

Go-Withs: *dinner rolls; wine, sparkling cider, coffee or tea*

recipe swaps

Any or all of the dishes on the Thanksgiving
menu on page 229 are suitable to serve for
Christmas dinner.

mixed greens with caramelized
walnuts and balsamic-pear vinaigrette

Caramelized walnuts add flavor and texture to this delicious salad that matches well with the luscious pear vinaigrette. Ribbons of sun-dried tomato accent the lettuce for a festive touch.

2 tablespoons plus 1 teaspoon
  light brown sugar
1 tablespoon vegan margarine
½ cup raw walnut halves
1 medium ripe Anjou pear
1 teaspoon fresh lemon juice
1 small shallot, coarsely
  chopped
2 tablespoons balsamic vinegar

¼ teaspoon salt
⅛ teaspoon dry mustard
⅛ teaspoon ground cayenne
¼ cup olive oil
6 cups mixed greens
4 oil-packed sun-dried tomato
  halves, cut into ⅛-inch-wide
  strips

1. In a small skillet, combine the 2 tablespoons sugar and the margarine and cook over medium heat, stirring until the sugar dissolves and the margarine is melted. Add the walnuts, stirring gently until the nuts are coated with the glaze. Quickly transfer the nuts to a nonstick baking sheet and spread in a single layer. Set aside to cool completely.

2. Cut the pear in half lengthwise. Rub the cut side of one pear half with the lemon juice and set aside. Peel and core the remaining pear half and place it in a food processor. Add the shallot, vinegar, remaining 1 teaspoon sugar, salt, mustard, and cayenne and process until smooth. Add the oil and process until well incorporated. Taste and adjust the seasonings, if necessary. Set aside.

3. In a large bowl, combine the greens, sun-dried tomatoes, and caramelized walnuts. Core the remaining pear half and cut it into paper-thin slices. Add the pear to the salad along with enough of the dressing to lightly coat. Toss gently to combine and serve.

make ahead   **quick & easy**

porcini-stuffed seitan with wild mushroom sauce

MAKES 6 TO 8 SERVINGS

The rich flavor of porcini mushrooms, featured in both the stuffing and the sauce, is the hallmark of this elegant roast that makes a delicious centerpiece on your holiday dinner table.

Note: *To make your own porcini powder, place one or two dried porcini in a spice grinder and grind to a powder. Store any unused porcini powder in an airtight container, where it will keep for several months.*

▪ STUFFING

3 dried porcini mushrooms
2 tablespoons olive oil
1 medium yellow onion, minced
1 celery rib, minced
2 garlic cloves, minced
2 cups coarsely chopped white
  mushrooms
1 teaspoon dried thyme
½ teaspoon dried sage
½ cup water
1 teaspoon salt
¼ teaspoon freshly ground black
  pepper
1½ cups cooked brown rice
3 cups fresh bread cubes, finely
  chopped
¼ cup minced fresh parsley

▪ SEITAN

2 cups vital wheat gluten
  (wheat gluten flour)
¼ cup nutritional yeast
1 teaspoon porcini powder (see
  note above)

¾ teaspoon onion powder
¾ teaspoon salt
½ teaspoon garlic powder
½ teaspoon sweet paprika
1½ cups cold water
¼ cup soy sauce
2 tablespoons olive oil plus
  more for rubbing

▪ SAUCE

1 tablespoon olive oil
3 tablespoons minced shallot
2 cups assorted fresh mushrooms, lightly rinsed, patted
  dry, and cut into ¼-inch slices
1 teaspoon minced fresh thyme
  leaves, or ½ teaspoon dried
2 cups vegetable broth
2 tablespoons soy sauce
1 tablespoon minced fresh parsley
Salt and freshly ground black
  pepper
2 tablespoons cornstarch
¼ cup water
½ teaspoon browning liquid

1. Make the stuffing: Place the dried porcini in a heatproof bowl and cover with boiling water. Set aside for 20 minutes to soften.

2. In a large skillet, heat the oil over medium heat. Add the onion and celery. Cover and cook until soft, about 10 minutes. Stir in the garlic, mushrooms, thyme, sage, water, salt, and pepper. Cook until the mushrooms release their juices, about 3 minutes. Remove from heat and set aside.

3. Drain the soaked porcini and finely chop. Stir them into the onion and mushroom mixture and transfer to a large bowl. Add the rice, bread and parsley and mix well, adding a little more water if the stuffing is too dry. Taste and adjust seasonings, if necessary. Refrigerate to cool completely while you make the seitan.

4. Make the seitan: In a food processor, combine the vital wheat gluten, yeast, porcini powder, onion powder, salt, garlic powder, and paprika. Pulse to blend. Add the water, soy sauce, and oil and process for a minute to form a soft dough. Turn the mixture out onto a lightly floured work surface and stretch it out with lightly floured hands until it is flat and about ½ inch thick. Place the flattened seitan between two sheets of plastic wrap or parchment paper. Use a rolling pin to flatten it as much as you can (it will be elastic and resistant). Top with a baking sheet weighed down with canned goods and let it rest for 10 minutes. Preheat the oven to 350°F.

5. When the stuffing is completely cool, place it in the center of the seitan and use your hands to press the stuffing into a firm log. Roll the seitan up and around the stuffing, using your fingers to seal the ends and the seam. Place the seitan on a large sheet of foil and roll it up, twisting the ends to seal. Place the wrapped seitan in a deep baking pan. Pour hot water into the pan about halfway up the sides of the seitan. Cover the pan tightly with foil and bake for 40 minutes.

6. Lightly grease a separate large baking pan. Remove the seitan from the water and remove the foil. Place the seitan in the prepared baking pan. Rub a little oil on the top and sides of the seitan and bake until firm and glossy brown, about 20 minutes.

7. Make the sauce: In a large saucepan, heat the oil over medium heat. Add the shallot and cook until soft, about 5 minutes. Add the mushrooms and cook 2 minutes longer. Add the thyme, broth, soy sauce, parsley, and salt and pepper, to taste. Bring to a boil. In a small bowl, combine the cornstarch and water and mix until blended. Reduce the heat to low, whisk the cornstarch mixture into the sauce, and stir until it thickens, about 3 minutes. Stir in the browning liquid. Taste and adjust seasonings, if necessary. If not using right away, bring to room temperature, then cover and refrigerate for up to 3 days.

8. Remove the seitan from the oven and set aside for 10 minutes before slicing. Use a serrated knife to cut most of it into ½-inch slices, leaving about one-third of it whole. Arrange the seitan on a large platter and pour some of the mushroom sauce on top. Serve hot with the remaining mushroom sauce at the table.

Note: *If you're planning to make this roast ahead of time (up to a day in advance), do not slice it. Instead, let it come to room temperature after baking, then cover and refrigerate until needed. The roast will cut more easily (and in neater slices) when chilled. Once sliced, you can then reassemble the roast and wrap it tightly in foil before reheating in the oven.*

herb-mashed potatoes

MAKES 4 TO 6 SERVINGS

Mashed potatoes are a holiday dinner tradition in many homes and this version is extra-special, made with buttery Yukon gold potatoes and seasoned with garlic and fresh herbs.

2 pounds Yukon gold potatoes

3 garlic cloves, crushed

2 fresh thyme sprigs

Salt

½ cup plain unsweetened soy milk or other nondairy milk

¼ cup vegan margarine

3 tablespoons minced fresh chives

3 tablespoons minced fresh parsley

1 tablespoon minced fresh tarragon (optional)

1. Peel the potatoes, if desired, and cut them into 2-inch chunks. Place the potatoes in a large pot with the garlic, thyme, and enough salted water to cover. Bring to a boil, then reduce the heat to medium-low, cover, and simmer until the potatoes are soft when pierced, 20 to 25 minutes. Remove the thyme sprigs and discard.

2. In a small saucepan, heat the soy milk and margarine over medium heat until the margarine is melted.

3. Drain the potatoes well, then return to the pot. Add the chives, parsley, tarragon, if using, and ½ teaspoon salt. Mash with a potato masher, stirring in the hot soy milk mixture a little at a time. Serve hot.

make ahead   quick & easy

wilted baby spinach with dried cranberries

MAKES 4 SERVINGS

Christmas colors never tasted so good, with this lovely sauté of baby spinach dotted with sweet-tart dried cranberries.

2 tablespoons olive oil
1 medium shallot, minced
1 pound fresh baby spinach

Salt and freshly ground black pepper
¼ cup dried cranberries

1. In a large skillet, heat the oil over medium heat. Add the shallot and cook until softened, about 3 minutes.

2. Add the spinach and season with salt and pepper, to taste. Cook, stirring, until the spinach is wilted, about 5 minutes. Stir in the cranberries. Serve hot.

an easter menu

At my house, Easter dinner is usually a variation of our Christmas dinner, but it features spring vegetables instead of winter vegetables.

To transform the Christmas menu into one more suited to Easter, simply substitute a seasonal vegetable such as roasted asparagus for the spinach with cranberries and serve new potatoes (either roasted or steamed) instead of mashed potatoes. Other menu changes might include swapping out the salad for the Baby Greens with Lemony Vinaigrette (page 250). For dessert, you could make the Fresh Berry Tartlets (page 97) instead of the apple tart.

spiced two-apple tart with cider crème

Mom's apple pie gets an update with this classy tart made with two kinds of apples and a creamy and luscious cider sauce.

CRUST

1½ cups all-purpose flour

½ cup vegan margarine, cut into pieces

1 teaspoon sugar

¼ teaspoon salt

¼ cup cold water

FILLING

3 Granny Smith apples

3 Rome or other red-skinned apples

½ teaspoon ground cinnamon

3 tablespoons sugar

2 tablespoons cold vegan margarine, cut into pieces

⅓ cup apple jelly, melted and kept warm

CIDER CRÈME

⅓ cup apple cider or juice

¼ cup light brown sugar

1 tablespoon pure maple syrup

½ teaspoon pure vanilla extract

½ cup vegan cream cheese, softened

1. Make the crust: In a food processor, combine the flour, margarine, sugar, and salt and pulse until crumbly. With the machine running, add the water and process to form a dough ball. Remove the dough, flatten into a disk about 1 inch thick, wrap it in plastic wrap, and refrigerate for 30 minutes.

2. Roll the dough out into a 12-inch circle on a lightly floured work surface. Transfer the dough to a lightly greased 10-inch tart pan with a removable bottom, fluted quiche pan, or pie plate, pressing evenly with your fingers to fit it into the pan and trimming the edges. Preheat the oven to 400°F.

3. Make the filling: Peel and core the apples and cut them into halves. Cut the apples into very thin slices. Spread about half of the apple slices evenly over the surface of the piecrust. Sprinkle with the cinnamon and 1 tablespoon of the sugar. Arrange the remaining apple slices overlapping in concentric circles, beginning with the outer circle and working toward the center. Sprinkle the remaining 2 tablespoons sugar on top of the apples, dot with bits of the margarine, and bake until the crust is cooked through and the apples are tender, about 45 minutes. Remove from the oven and brush the top of the tart with the apple jelly. Cool for at least 30 minutes before serving.

4. Make the cider crème: In a medium saucepan, combine the cider, sugar, and maple syrup. Bring just to a boil over medium-high heat, stirring constantly. Reduce the heat to medium-low and cook, stirring, for about 2 minutes to blend the flavors. Remove from the heat and stir in the vanilla. Place the softened cream cheese in a bowl. Add the hot cider mixture in batches, stirring to blend after each addition. Stir until well blended and smooth. To serve, cut the tart into slices, plate, and top with the cider crème. The tart may be made several hours in advance and covered and stored at room temperature. It tastes best if eaten on the same day as it is made.

make ahead   **quick & easy**

hanukkah

This festive Jewish holiday is celebrated over eight days; during this time candles are lit on the menorah, small gifts are exchanged, blessings are recited, and traditional games are played. This eight-day festival of lights is also a time for wonderful meals. With traditional dishes like crisp potato latkes, new favorites such as stuffed portobello mushrooms, and a new riff on rugalach for dessert, even non-vegan family members will enjoy this delicious menu. Of course, there's no need to reserve these recipes for Hanukkah alone—they can be enjoyed on any occasion.

the menu

HANUKKAH MENU
Baby Greens with Lemony Vinaigrette
Quinoa-Stuffed Portobello Mushrooms
*   with Wine-Braised Shallots*
Potato Latkes with Cranberry-Apple Relish
Tarragon Green Beans with Toasted Pine Nuts
Chocolate-Raspberry Rugalach

Go-Withs: *wine, sparkling cider, coffee or tea*

baby greens with lemony vinaigrette

MAKES 4 SERVINGS

This crisp green salad is dressed with a creamy vinaigrette made with fresh lemon juice. It makes a refreshing start to the Hanukkah meal.

2 tablespoons unsalted raw cashews

1 garlic clove, crushed

3 tablespoons fresh lemon juice

2 tablespoons water

2 teaspoons nutritional yeast

1 teaspoon agave nectar

½ teaspoon salt

⅛ teaspoon freshly ground black pepper

¼ cup olive oil

5 to 6 cups mixed baby greens

1. In a high-speed blender, grind the cashews to a fine powder. Add the garlic, lemon juice, and water and blend until smooth. Add the yeast, agave nectar, salt, pepper, and oil. Blend until smooth and creamy.

2. Place the greens in a large bowl. Add the dressing, toss gently to coat, and serve.

quinoa-stuffed portobello mushrooms
with wine-braised shallots

MAKES 4 SERVINGS

This elegant main dish can be assembled ahead of time for easy serving. Choose large portobello mushroom caps to make a substantial serving.

4 large portobello mushrooms, lightly rinsed and patted dry

2 tablespoons olive oil

3 large shallots, chopped

2 garlic cloves, minced

⅓ cup plus 2 tablespoons dry white wine

1 teaspoon minced fresh thyme or ½ teaspoon dried

Salt and freshly ground black pepper

1¼ cups cooked quinoa

2 tablespoons minced fresh parsley

1 tablespoon nutritional yeast

1. Carefully remove the stems from the mushrooms and set the mushroom caps aside. Wash the stems well, chop them, and set aside. Preheat the oven to 375°F. Lightly grease a 9 × 13-inch baking pan and set aside.

2. In a large skillet, heat 1 tablespoon of the oil over medium heat. Add the shallots and garlic. Cover and cook until softened, about 3 minutes. Uncover and stir in the chopped mushroom stems, the ⅓ cup wine, thyme, and salt and pepper, to taste. Simmer to blend the flavors and reduce the liquid, about 5 minutes. Remove from the heat, stir in the quinoa, parsley, and yeast. Mix to combine well, then taste and adjust the seasonings, if necessary.

3. Use the edge of a teaspoon to scrape out and discard the brown gills from the underside of the mushroom caps. Carefully spoon the stuffing mixture into the mushroom caps, packing them tightly and smoothing the tops.

4. Transfer the stuffed mushrooms to the prepared pan and drizzle with the remaining 1 tablespoon oil. Pour the remaining 2 tablespoons wine in the pan, cover tightly with foil, and bake until the mushrooms are tender and the stuffing is hot, about 20 minutes. Uncover and cook until the stuffing is lightly browned, about 10 minutes longer. Serve hot.

make ahead   **quick & easy**

potato latkes with cranberry-apple relish

MAKES 4 TO 6 SERVINGS

Food prepared in oil is a Hanukkah tradition to commemorate the miracle of the oil that burned for eight days. Potato latkes are a favorite and delicious way to observe this tradition. For the Cranberry-Apple Relish, see page 235.

1½ pounds Yukon gold potatoes

⅓ cup shredded yellow onion

3 tablespoons finely shredded carrot

2 tablespoons minced fresh parsley

¼ cup all-purpose flour

½ teaspoon baking powder

1 teaspoon salt

¼ teaspoon freshly ground black pepper

Neutral vegetable oil, for frying

Cranberry-Apple Relish (page 235)

1. Peel and grate the potatoes and place them in a colander set over a large bowl. Use your hands to squeeze all the liquid from the potatoes. Discard the liquid. Transfer the squeezed potatoes to a large bowl. Add the onion, carrot, parsley, flour, baking powder, salt, and pepper and mix well.

2. Preheat the oven to 250°F. In a large skillet, heat a thin layer of oil over medium heat. Press flat a heaping tablespoon of the potato mixture, then gently place in the hot oil. Repeat this process with the remaining mixture and add to the pan, a few at a time, to avoid crowding. Fry until golden brown on both sides, turning once, about 8 minutes total. Remove the cooked latkes to a heatproof platter and keep warm in the oven while you cook the rest. Serve immediately with the Cranberry-Apple Relish.

tarragon green beans with toasted pine nuts

MAKES 4 SERVINGS

Fragrant tarragon, garlic, and crunchy toasted pine nuts elevate these green beans from simple side dish to simply sensational.

1 pound green beans, trimmed
¼ cup pine nuts
2 tablespoons olive oil
2 garlic cloves, minced

1 tablespoon coarsely chopped fresh tarragon
Salt and freshly ground black pepper

1. Steam the green beans until just tender, about 7 minutes. Rinse under cold water and set aside.

2. In a large dry skillet, toast the pine nuts over medium heat, stirring so they don't burn, about 4 minutes. Remove from the skillet and set aside.

3. In the same skillet, heat the oil over medium heat. Add the garlic and cook until fragrant, about 30 seconds. Add the steamed green beans and cook, stirring occasionally, for 1 minute. Add the tarragon, toasted pine nuts, and salt and pepper, to taste. Cook, stirring, for 1 minute to heat through and blend the flavors. Serve hot.

make ahead   **quick & easy**

chocolate-raspberry rugalach

MAKES 3 DOZEN COOKIES

This menu features a delicious variation on rugalach, a classic cookie that can be enjoyed anytime.

1½ cups all-purpose flour
½ cup plus 3 tablespoons sugar
3 tablespoons unsweetened
  cocoa powder
¼ teaspoon salt
¾ cup vegan cream cheese,
  softened
½ cup vegan margarine,

softened
¾ teaspoon pure vanilla extract
½ cup ground pecans
½ teaspoon ground cinnamon
¾ cup seedless raspberry jam
1 tablespoon plain or vanilla soy
  milk or other nondairy milk

1. In a food processor, combine the flour, ½ cup of the sugar, cocoa, and salt, and process until well combined. Cut the cream cheese and margarine into quarters and add them to the flour mixture. Add the vanilla and process until well blended and the mixture becomes a soft dough ball, adding a little flour if the dough is too sticky. Turn the dough out onto a lightly floured work surface and divide into 3 equal pieces. Pat each piece of dough into a disk, wrap each disk in plastic, and chill for about 1 hour.

2. In a medium bowl, combine the pecans, 2 tablespoons of the sugar, and the cinnamon until well mixed. Set aside. Preheat the oven to 350°F. Grease a large baking sheet or line it with parchment paper and set aside.

3. On a lightly floured work surface, with a floured rolling pin, roll out 1 piece of the chilled dough into an 8- to 9-inch round, keeping the remaining dough refrigerated. Spread the dough with ¼ cup of the raspberry jam, then sprinkle on one-third of the pecan mixture.

4. Using a sharp knife or pastry wheel, cut the dough round into 12 equal wedges. Starting at the wide edge, roll up each wedge into a small crescent. Place the cookies on the prepared baking sheet, about ½ inch apart, point side down. Repeat with the remaining dough and filling ingredients. Use a pastry brush to brush the cookies with the soy milk, then sprinkle with the remaining 1 tablespoon sugar. Bake until lightly browned, about 20 minutes. Immediately remove to wire racks to cool. When cool, store at room temperature in an airtight container.

M make ahead   quick & easy

hanukkah

new year's eve a-list

The "A" stands for "appetizers," and this party provides a host of savory pickup foods when an arsenal of tasty bites is in order. These recipes can be made in advance and are easily mixed and matched with crudités and dips along with other nibbles for informal gatherings. You can also choose just one of these recipes to serve with drinks prior to a sit-down meal.

A New Year's Eve party involves noisemakers, lots of food and drink, and a champagne toast at midnight. Some people make New Year's Eve a costume party or have some other theme. A well-known custom in the southern United States is hoppin' John, which is made with black-eyed peas and rice and served with collard greens on New Year's Day. It's said to bring good fortune in the coming year. Consider getting those one-cup plastic containers and filling them with hoppin' John as a party favor for your guests to bring home for an auspicious beginning to the New Year.

the menu

NEW YEAR'S EVE NOSHES AND NIBBLES

Spinach Phyllo Cigars with Walnuts and Figs
Artichoke-Stuffed Mushrooms
Truffled White Bean Hummus
Polenta Crostini with Eggplant Tapenade
Pastry-Wrapped Stuffed Cherry Peppers

Go-Withs: nuts, chips, crackers, breads, olives; wine, champagne, punch

recipe swaps

If you'd like to swap out any of the appetizers in this menu, or perhaps add an item or two if you're expecting extra people, here are some items that will fit the bill:

Artichoke Tapenade (page 38)

Sun-Dried Tomato and Green Olive Biscotti (page 39)

Chickpea-Artichoke Bites with Rosemary Aïoli (page 153)

Black Olive Tapenade with Carrot Sticks and Orange Bell Pepper Strips (page 223)

Baked Potato Skins (page 110); or Zucchini Cups with Tomato Concassé (page 63)

last-minute rescue

A BACKUP PLAN FOR ANY PARTY

Although they are listed as Go-Withs on this menu, having a supply of nuts, chips, olives, crackers, and breads can also provide a buffer in case you run out of one or more of your appetizers. Estimating how many appetizers you'll need for a party is not an exact science, and if your guests are especially ravenous, you'll be glad you have some backup food on hand.

spinach phyllo cigars with walnuts and figs

MAKES 2 DOZEN CIGARS

This crunchy appetizer is easy to assemble and can be made ahead so it is ready to bake at party time. Pine nuts may be substituted for the walnuts, if desired.

2 tablespoons olive oil plus
  more for brushing
3 garlic cloves, minced
½ cup finely chopped walnuts
½ cup finely chopped figs
4 cups fresh baby spinach
1 cup cooked or white beans,
  drained, rinsed, and mashed

2 tablespoons coarsely chopped
  fresh parsley
2 teaspoons finely grated
  lemon zest
Salt and freshly ground black
  pepper
4 sheets phyllo pastry, thawed

1. In a large skillet, heat 2 tablespoons of the oil over medium heat. Add the garlic and cook until fragrant. Add the walnuts, figs, and spinach and cook, stirring, until the spinach is wilted. Stir in the beans, parsley, and zest and season with salt and pepper, to taste. Transfer to a bowl and mix well. Set aside until cool.

2. Place a sheet of phyllo dough on a flat work surface. Keep the remaining dough covered with plastic wrap to keep from drying out. Lightly brush the phyllo with oil, then using a sharp knife, cut the phyllo sheet into 4 strips. Spoon about 2 tablespoons of the filling along the bottom edge of 1 strip of phyllo, then tightly roll up to enclose the filling, tucking in the ends. Transfer the phyllo cigar to a platter.

3. Repeat the process for the remaining phyllo until the filling is used up. When all of the phyllo cigars are assembled, cover tightly with plastic wrap and refrigerate for at least 30 minutes.

4. Preheat the oven to 425°F. Transfer the phyllo cigars to a nonstick cookie sheet and bake until golden brown, about 15 minutes. Serve hot. If not using right away, refrigerate overnight or freeze for up to 2 weeks.

make ahead   **quick & easy**

artichoke-stuffed mushrooms

The sublime flavor combination of artichokes and mushrooms make this easy and elegant appetizer a stand-out at any gathering. If you make the stuffed mushrooms ahead of time, they can be ready to bake when needed.

1 (10-ounce) package frozen artichoke hearts or 1 (15-ounce) can unmarinated artichoke hearts, drained

16 ounces white mushrooms, lightly rinsed and patted dry

2 tablespoons olive oil

2 garlic cloves, minced

2 tablespoons minced fresh parsley

½ teaspoon Dijon mustard

½ teaspoon dried thyme

½ teaspoon salt

¼ teaspoon freshly ground black pepper

½ cup dry bread crumbs

1. If using frozen artichoke hearts, cook them in a small saucepan of boiling salted water until tender, about 10 minutes. Drain well and run under cold water to cool. Finely chop the artichokes and set aside.

2. Remove the stems from the mushrooms and set aside. In a large skillet, heat the oil over medium heat. Add the mushroom caps and cook until softened slightly, 2 to 3 minutes. Remove from the skillet and set aside. Preheat the oven to 400°F. Lightly grease a large baking pan and set aside.

3. Finely chop the mushroom stems and add to the same skillet. Add the garlic and cook over medium heat until softened, about 2 minutes. Add the chopped artichoke hearts, parsley, mustard, thyme, salt, and pepper. Cook for 2 minutes, stirring well to combine. Stir in the bread crumbs, mixing well.

4. Fill the mushroom caps with the stuffing mixture and arrange in the baking pan. Bake until the filling is hot and the mushrooms are tender, about 10 minutes. Serve hot. If not using right away, the stuffed mushrooms may be covered and refrigerated overnight, then baked when ready to serve.

260

truffled white bean hummus

Traditional chickpea hummus is so "last year"—ring in the New Year with this creamy white bean variation made sophisticated (and delicious) with a touch of truffle oil and chives.

2 garlic cloves, crushed
½ teaspoon salt
1½ cups cooked or 1
   (15.5-ounce) can white beans,
   drained and rinsed
1 tablespoon finely minced
   fresh chives

2 tablespoons fresh lemon juice
1 tablespoon plus 1 teaspoon
   truffle oil
½ teaspoon black sesame seeds,
   for garnish

1. In a food processor, process the garlic and salt until finely minced. Add the beans, chives, and lemon juice and process until smooth.

2. With the machine running, stream in the 1 tablespoon oil and process until smooth. Taste and adjust seasonings, if necessary. Transfer to a medium bowl, cover, and refrigerate for 2 hours or up to 24 hours before serving. Before serving, drizzle with the remaining 1 teaspoon oil and garnish with black sesame seeds.

make ahead   **quick & easy**

polenta crostini with eggplant tapenade

Slices of polenta stand in for bread in this crostini appetizer topped with a luscious eggplant tapenade. Like the other recipes in this chapter, this recipe can be made ahead, leaving just the last-minute heating of the polenta.

POLENTA

3 cups water or vegetable broth

Salt

1 cup polenta cornmeal
   (medium to coarse ground)

1 tablespoon olive oil

Salt and freshly ground black
   pepper

TAPENADE

1 large eggplant

½ cup pitted kalamata olives

1 tablespoon capers, drained

3 garlic cloves

3 tablespoons olive oil

Salt and freshly ground black
   pepper

1. Make the polenta: In a large saucepan, bring the water to a boil over high heat. Salt the water and slowly stream in the polenta, whisking constantly. Reduce the heat to low and continue whisking until the polenta thickens and pulls away from the sides of the saucepan, about 15 minutes. Stir in the oil and season with salt and pepper, to taste. Smooth into a greased loaf pan and refrigerate for at least 1 hour.

2. Make the tapenade: Preheat the oven to 425°F. Coat the eggplant lightly with oil and place it on a baking sheet. Roast the eggplant for 20 minutes, or until the skin is blistered and brown. Set aside and peel when cool enough to handle.

3. In a food processor, combine the roasted eggplant, olives, capers, and garlic and pulse until coarsely chopped. Add the oil and salt and pepper, to taste, and pulse to mix well. Transfer the tapenade to a small serving bowl and set aside. Preheat the oven to 350°F.

4. Cut the chilled polenta into ½-inch-thick slices (you may cut them into smaller shapes with a knife or cookie cutter, if you wish) and arrange them on a greased baking sheet. Bake until golden, about 15 minutes. To serve, place the bowl of tapenade in the center of a platter and surround with the polenta. If not using right away, the tapenade may be tightly wrapped and refrigerated for up to 3 days. The polenta may be kept tightly wrapped in the loaf pan for up to 2 days, and then sliced and baked when ready to serve.

make ahead   quick & easy

pastry-wrapped stuffed cherry peppers

MAKES ABOUT 20 PEPPERS

Zesty stuffed peppers cloaked in pastry make an elegant and easy appetizer boasting a great variety of flavors and textures in a small package. Look for cherry peppers in well-stocked supermarkets or Italian grocery stores. Try to find jars containing smallish peppers (around 1 inch in diameter). If the ones you have are larger, cut them in half for stuffing to make them a more manageable size.

1 (16-ounce) jar hot or mild cherry peppers, drained

2 tablespoons olive oil

2 garlic cloves, minced

2 cups finely chopped white mushrooms

½ cup pine nuts

½ cup coarsely chopped sun-dried tomatoes

½ cup fresh unseasoned bread crumbs

1 teaspoon dried basil

Salt and freshly ground black pepper

2 frozen vegan puff pastry sheets, thawed

1. Preheat the oven to 400°F. Lightly grease a 9 x 13-inch baking pan and set aside. Slice the tops off the cherry peppers, scrape out the seeds, and set aside.

2. In a large skillet, heat the oil over medium heat. Add the garlic and cook 30 seconds. Add the mushrooms and cook until softened, about 4 minutes. Stir in the pine nuts and cook for 1 minute. Set aside to cool completely.

3. Transfer the mushroom mixture to a food processor and add the sun-dried tomatoes, bread crumbs, basil, and salt and pepper, to taste. Pulse until well combined. Stuff the cherry peppers with the mixture and set aside.

4. Unfold the pastry sheet onto a lightly floured work surface and roll into a rectangle about 12 x 15 inches. Use a sharp knife or pizza cutter to cut the pastry into 3- to 3½-inch squares. Lightly flour your hands to keep the pastry from sticking to them. Place a stuffed pepper in the center of a pastry square and use your hands to enclose the pepper in the pastry, smoothing with your fingers to shape it into a smooth sphere. Place on the prepared baking sheet and repeat with the remaining peppers and pastry. Refrigerate for about 10 minutes to firm up or until ready to use. (You can assemble the pastry-wrapped peppers up to 24 hours in advance.) Bake until golden brown, about 12 minutes. Serve warm or at room temperature. These can be made several hours in advance and stored at room temperature. To serve, crisp in a preheated 400° F oven for 2 to 3 minutes.

make ahead   quick & easy

recipes by category
(make ahead; quick & easy)

M **make ahead** (means it can be prepared and stored in advance)
Q **quick & easy** (means ready in less than 20 minutes)

hors d'oeuvres	make ahead	quick & easy
Artichoke Tapenade	M	Q
Sun-Dried Tomato and Green Olive Biscotti	M	
Olive-cado Dip		Q
Finger-Lickin' Tempeh Fingers	M	
Chickpea-Artichoke Bites with Rosemary Aïoli	M	
Collard and Red Bean Fritters	M	
Spinach-Potato Quesadillas	M	
Chorizo en Croûte	M	
Vegetable Dippers with Ranch Dressing	M	Q
It's My Party Mix	M	
Mutant Ants on a Log	M	Q
Mini Blue Corn Pancakes with Chipotle-Streaked Sour Cream	M	Q
Curried Pakora Puffs	M	
Black Olive Tapenade with Carrot Sticks and Orange Bell Pepper Strips	M	Q
Baked Potato Skins	M	
Five-Story Bean Dip	M	Q
Sherried Mushrooms	M	Q
Olive-and-Caper-Stuffed Cherry Tomatoes	M	Q
Pearl Balls		

	make ahead	quick & easy
Spinach Phyllo Cigars with Walnuts and Figs	M	
Artichoke-Stuffed Mushrooms	M	
Polenta Crostini with Eggplant Tapenade	M	
Truffled White Bean Hummus	M	Q
Pastry-Wrapped Stuffed Cherry Peppers	M	
Fava Bean Hummus	M	Q
Smoky Baba Ghanoush	M	
Spiced Pita Dippers	M	Q
Mini Falafel	M	
Stuffed Dates	M	Q
Edamame	M	Q
Japanese Pancakes (Okonomiyaki)	M	
Teriyaki Shiitake Sticks	M	
Sushi Rice Balls	M	
Gingered "Crab" Cups with Wasabi Cream Cheese	M	
Antipasto Skewers	M	
Grilled Vegetable Skewers	M	
Mini Focaccia with Tapenade	M	
Zucchini Cups with Tomato Concassé	M	
Arugula and White Bean Crostini	M	
Pesto-Stuffed Baby Potatoes		Q

soups

	make ahead	quick & easy
Red Bliss Potato and Fennel Soup	M	
Pea Green Soup	M	
Cousin Jenny's Matzo Ball Soup	M	
Chestnut Bisque	M	
Hot and Sour Soup	M	

salads

	make ahead	quick & easy
Butterhead and Radicchio Salad with Walnut-Pesto Dressing		Q
Super Slaw	M	Q
Shamrock Vegetable Salad		Q
Romaine and Avocado Salad with Cilantro-Cumin Vinaigrette		Q
Strawberry Carpaccio with Balsamic Syrup		Q
Three-Potato Salad	M	

recipesby**category**

	make ahead	quick & easy
Herbed Vegetable Salad	M	Q
Fingerling Potato Salad with Pan-Fried Arugula Pesto	M	
Black Rice Salad	M	
Spanish Orange Salad	M	Q
Mixed Greens with Caramelized Walnuts and Balsamic-Pear Vinaigrette		Q
Baby Greens with Lemony Vinaigrette		Q

main dishes

	make ahead	quick & easy
Wild Mushroom Ragu over Polenta	M	
Devil's Details Chili	M	
Pastry-Wrapped Seitan Roulades with Spinach-Mushroom Duxelles	M	
Colcannon-Topped Irish Stew	M	
Smoke and Spice Jambalaya	M	
Roasted Eggplant and Potato Torta	M	
Seitan Enchiladas with Mole Poblano	M	
Asparagus Quiche-Me-Not	M	
Spicy-Smoky BBQ Ribz	M	
Personal Pizzas	M	
Independence Burgers	M	
Mixed Vegetable Curry	M	
Southern Fried Seitan	M	Q
Black Bean and Butternut Chili	M	
Baked Potato Skins	M	
Seitan Buffalo Wingz	M	
Ultimate Taco Bar	M	Q
Buttercup Squash Stuffed with Wild Rice, Shiitake Mushrooms, and Caramelized Leeks	M	
Porcini-Stuffed Seitan with Wild Mushroom Sauce	M	
Quinoa-Stuffed Portobello Mushrooms with Wine-Braised Shallots	M	
Spiced Chickpea and Couscous Pilaf	M	Q
Very Veggie Lasagna	M	
Two-Potato Shepherd's Pie	M	
Creamy Noodle and Vegetable Bake	M	
Antipasto Rice	M	Q
Pan-Fried Sesame Noodles and Broccoli		Q
Brown Rice with Pineapple and Green Onions	M	Q
Caramelized Tofu	M	Q

recipesby**category**

	make ahead	quick & easy
Orange-Kissed Chocolate Tiramisù	M	
Man-Size Chocolate Chip Cookies	M	
Chocolate-Cherry Cheesecake	M	
Creamy Lime-Pistachio Parfaits	M	Q
Pastry-Wrapped Bananas Foster	M	
Fruit Crisp with Matzo Crumb Topping	M	
Tres Leches Cupcakes	M	
Chocolate "Pots de Crème"	M	Q
Blueberry-Peach Cobbler	M	
Build-Your-Own Ice Cream Sundaes	M	
Mixed Berry Crumble	M	
Cardamom Rice Pudding	M	
Caramel Almond-Oat Bars	M	
Orange-Carrot Cake with Dark Chocolate Icing	M	
Everyone's Favorite Ice Cream Cake	M	Q
Pecan-Pumpkin Pie	M	
Spiced Two-Apple Tart with Cider Crème	M	
Chocolate-Raspberry Rugalach	M	
Chocolate Lover's Brownies	M	
Pine Nut–Anise Cookies	M	
Pistachio-Dusted Chocolate-Raspberry Truffles	M	
Ginger-Spice Cupcakes	M	
Fresh Berry Tartlets	M	
Fresh Fruit Picks with Two Dips	M	Q
Coconut Snowballs	M	Q
Cherry-Pecan Bars	M	
Italian Wedding Cookies	M	
Chocolate Chunk Blondies	M	
Strawberries Dipped in Chocolate	M	Q

index

index

273

index

index